◆

All of us here will gradually disappear if
no one searches for us, if no one names us

# mpT
## MODERN POETRY
## IN TRANSLATION
*The best of world poetry*

No. 2 2021
© *Modern Poetry in Translation* 2021 and contributors

ISSN (print) 0969-3572
ISSN (online) 2052-3017
ISBN (print) 978-1-910485-30-9

Editor: Clare Pollard
Managing Editor: Sarah Hesketh
Digital Content Editor: Ed Cottrell
Finance Manager: Deborah De Kock
Design by Jenny Flynn
Cover art by Sofia Rosales
Typesetting by Libanus Press

Printed and bound in Great Britain by Charlesworth Press, Wakefield
For submissions and subscriptions please visit
www.modernpoetryintranslation.com

Modern Poetry in Translation Limited. A Company Limited by Guarantee
Registered in England and Wales, Number 5881603
UK Registered Charity Number 1118223

Supported using public funding by
## ARTS COUNCIL
## ENGLAND

*Modern Poetry in Translation* gratefully acknowledges the support
of The Polish Cultural Institute for working with us on the
Norwid 200 project, both in this issue and online.

POLISH CULTURAL
INSTITUTE
LONDON

# MODERN POETRY IN TRANSLATION

*If No One Names Us*

# CONTENTS

Editorial   **1**

INGER CHRISTENSEN, 'Butterfly Valley'   **3**
Translated by DAVID BROADBRIDGE

ELIN AP HYWEL, two poems   **14**
Translated by LAURA FISK

NILLANTHAN, three poems   **17**
Translated by GEETHA SUKUMARAN and SHASH TREVETT

## Norwid 200

Introduction by CLARE POLLARD   **22**

CYPRIAN KAMIL NORWID, 'The Last Despotism'   **23**
Translated by ADAM CZERNIAWSKI

MALIKA BOOKER, 'To Poet Cyprian Kamil Norwid'   **24**

WAYNE HOLLOWAY-SMITH, 'Rabbits'   **26**

ROMALYN ANTE, 'Forgetting'   **28**
Translated by ROMALYN ANTE

ENDRE RUSET, four poems   **31**
Translated by HARRY MAN

## Three Istrian Poets

Introduction by ANDRÉ NAFFIS-SAHELY   **36**

LIGIO ZANINI, 'Without a Name'   **37**
Translated by ANDRÉ NAFFIS-SAHELY

LIDIA DELTON, 'An Old Photograph'   **37**
Translated by ANDRÉ NAFFIS-SAHELY

LOREDANA BOGLIÙN, 'A Touch of Boùmbaro'   **38**
Translated by ANDRÉ NAFFIS-SAHELY

JACQUES BREL, 'Amsterdam'   **40**
Translated by PAUL RODDIE

JEAN-CLAUDE AWONO, two poems   **44**
Translated by GEORGINA COLLINS

# Focus

NAHUI OLIN, two poems  **48**
Translated by CLAIRE MULLEN

NATALIA TOLEDO, three poems  **52**
Translated by CLARE SULLIVAN and IRMA PINEDA

PITA AMOR, two poems  **55**
Translated by AMANDA HOPKINSON and NICK CAISTOR

JUANA ADCOCK, two poems  **61**
Translated by ROBIN MYERS

GUILLERMO FERNÁNDEZ, 'Dark-skinned Hand  **64**
on a White Tablecloth'
Translated by ADRIANA DIAZ-ENCISO

MIKEAS SÁNCHEZ, from Mokaya  **67**
Translated by WENDY CALL

MARTÍN TONALMEYOTL, 'Tierra de Perros'  **71**
Translated by WHITNEY DEVOS

MARTÍN RANGEL, two poems  **73**
Translated by LAWRENCE SCHIMEL

SARA URIBE, from Antígona González  **76**
Translated by JD PLUECKER

OSCAR DAVID LÓPEZ, two poems  **79**
Translated by LEO BOIX

ELENA PONIATOWSKA, 'Open Sky'  **82**
Translated by CYNTHIA STEELE

AMANDA HOPKINSON  **86**
Short interview with ELENA PONIATOWSKA
about Nursery Rhymes for a Naughty Girl

ELENA PONIATOWSKA, 'Guardian Angel'  **88**
Translated by AMANDA HOPKINSON & NICK CAISTOR

TEDI LÓPEZ MILLS, two poems  **90**
Translated by JS TENNANT

ENRIQUETA OCHOA, 'Power, War' **94**
Translated by ANTHONY SEIDMAN

JUANA KAREN PEÑATE, three poems **96**
Translated by WENDY CALL and SARAH VAN ARSDALE

JEANNETTE L CLARIOND, two poems **99**
Translated by SAMANTHA SCHNEE

## *Reviews*

We are the Land, KAREN MCCARTHY WOOLF **104**
A major anthology of indigenous poetries of North America

Forms of Resistance, STEPHANIE SY-QUIA **108**
Three pamphlets explore free and unfree bodies

The First Step of Day, CHARLIE LOUTH **112**
PHILIPPE JACCOTTET's 'attentive interrogation of the world'

NOTES ON CONTRIBUTORS **116**

# EDITORIAL

After long, dark months reading pandemic poems earlier this year, I was keen to pick a focus for the summer issue which would give me and our readers pleasure. The idea of a Focus on Mexico has been in my mind for a while – Mexico is one of my favourite countries, and over the last few years I have been lucky to publish many great Mexican poets, from Jimena González to Martha Mega; Hubert Matiúwàa to Claudia Berrueto. I sensed that a Mexican Focus would have my submission box overbrimming with spectacular poets, and so it has been. What a delight, to discover figures like Nahui Olin, widely known for her 'large green eyes and fiery spirit' in Mexico City in the 1920s and 30s – whose extraordinary poems, as translator Claire Mullen explains, cover everything from Einstein's theory of relativity to the discovery of black holes, 'sexuality, feminism, and Mexican nationality'. Or Pita Amor, who would turn up for her sittings as an artist's model for Diego Riviera 'nude beneath her mink coat', and whose poems were so original she became known as 'the 11th Muse of Mexico'.

There are some powerful poems by men in this focus, but it is the sheer number of brilliant women writing poetry in Mexico right now that has struck me, from the Zapotec poet Natalia Toledo's empathy with the turtle, weeping as she lays her eggs, to Mikeas Sanchez celebrating 'all the Zoque women's wisdom in my spit', to Elena Poniatowska declaring – in Cynthia Steele's memorable translation – that 'Sanctity is some incomprehensible shit'. Our cover, by Mexican illustrator Sofia Rosales, represents Coyolxauhqui, goddess of the moon, and is inspired by the poetry of Jeannette L Clariond's sequence *The Goddesses of Water* (soon to be published by Shearsman, translated by Samantha Schnee), where Coyolxauhqui's dismemberment by her brother, the sun, 'symbolises the successive phases of the Moon in endless darkness'. It tells of a journey out of chaos and violence towards light.

Many thanks, as ever, to our many friends who helped spread the word and gave me guidance, with a particular shout out to Amanda Hopkinson for all her help, Nathalie Teitler and Leo Boix of Nuevo Sol, and to James Byrne and the editors of the forthcoming *Temporary Archives: Latin American Women Poets* (Arc/EHUP), which will be essential reading. I hope you will all enjoy this focus as much as I do, along with the issue's many other pleasures – including poems in response to CK Norwid's centenary, a new translation of Jacques Brel's 'Amsterdam', and 'Butterfly Valley', a truly gorgeous sonnet redoublé by Inger Christensen, translated by David Broadbridge. It is poetry for warmer days, and to bring us back to ourselves: 'They are rising up, the earth's butterflies'.

# INGER CHRISTENSEN

Translated by David Broadbridge

'Butterfly Valley' is a sonnet redoublé – a sequence of fifteen sonnets where the last line of every sonnet is the first line of the next. The fifteenth 'master' sonnet is itself composed of all the first lines in order of the preceding fourteen sonnets. This presents a considerable challenge to a translator, particularly when the metrical and rhyme schemes are followed, which is essential if it is to do justice to the discipline of the form that the poem embodies.

This dialogue between author and translator means working with the rhythms and word order of speech, together with metre and rhyme, to make the poem in translation feel as natural as a poem originally written in English. As Edith Grossman says in *Why Translation Matters*: 'Fidelity to the effect and impact of the original is making the second version of the work as close to the first writer's intention as possible'.

As when I translated Danish Ballads, I took Seamus Heaney's description of translating *Beowulf* as my starting point: 'It is one thing to find lexical meanings for the words and to have some feel for how the metre might go, but it is quite another thing to find the tuning-fork that will give you the note and pitch for the overall music of the work'. With this in mind, my translation of 'Butterfly Valley' is an attempt at impersonation – to make Inger Christensen sound like herself in English.

## Butterfly Valley

### I

They are rising up, the earth's butterflies,
pigments from the warm body of the ground,
cinnabar, ochre, phosphor, gold, they rise,
a swarm of basic elements abound.

Is this fluttering of wings a seeming
throng of light particles, imagined sight?
Is it my childhood's summertime dreaming
splintered by the lightning of time-torn light?

No, this is light's angel, who can regale
himself as black Apollo's mnemosyne,
as Copper, Poplar Hawk-moth, Swallowtail.

I see them with blurred reason, incomplete
through a quilted haze of feathers so fine
in Brajcino Valley's high noonday heat.

### II

In Brajcino Valley's high noonday heat,
where memory fades, and all things in sight
in the coincidence of plants and light
are changed from scentlessness to scent so sweet,

there I return and move from leaf to leaf
place them in the nettles of childhood cares,
the most divine of all of nature's snares,
which captures what has flown in days so brief.

In its cocoon the Admiral repined,
from a greedy caterpillar grows there
changing itself to what we call a mind,

so that, like other summers' butterflies,
it brings the rich purple of life's hue, where
from bitter caverns underground they rise.

III
From bitter caverns underground they rise,
where the cellar-dark first dream-crawlers creep
and all cruelty we would rather hide,
are the depths that lie beneath the mind's deep,

up ascends Morpheus, the Death's-head, all,
that turn the Hawk-moth inside out, and what
they show me is how soft it is to fall,
into ash-greyness and resemble god.

From a Vejle meadow the Cabbage White,
the white soul whose painted wings awaken
and reflect the transience of our life,

what does it want here in this gloomy heat?
Is it the grief my life has overtaken,
hidden in scented mountain scrub so sweet?

**IV**

Hidden in scented mountain scrub so sweet,
that flowering is rooted in decay,
shadowful, entangled, in disarray,
a wild maze of madness incomplete,

the butterfly by fluttering conceals
that in an insect's body it's trapped tight,
you'd think it was a flower that took flight,
not the iconoclasm it reveals,

as when Carpet, Owl or Silk moth freely,
whirl the coloured characters in relief,
and throw to us a hidden mystery,

so all our thinking can look forward to
and beyond is the symmetry of grief
as Admiral, Camberwell Beauty, Blue.


**V**

As Admiral, Camberwell Beauty, Blue
in bright colour's periodic system
helped by the smallest nectar's droplet too,
can lift up the earth like a diadem,

as they in colour's carefree bright motif,
lavender, purple, lignite black, when caught
precisely fix the hiding-place of grief,
although their joy in life is all too short.

their probosces can still absorb it seems
the world as if a picture book of dreams,
as light as the touch of being caressed,

until all of love's gleams have been expressed,
though gleams of dread and beauty unbound vie,
as Peacock butterflies fluttering by.


## VI

As Peacock butterflies fluttering by,
I feel as if I walk in Paradise,
while the garden to nothing sinks to die,
and words that could be spelt out in a trice

melt into false eye rings on wings in flight,
the Copper, Burgundy and Harlequin,
whose conjured words each silicon-white night
transform the light of day to moonlight thin.

Here you can find the gooseberry and sloe,
indifferent to which words you will gainsay
making your life butterfly-light to know.

Should I perhaps pupate myself and drool
at all white Harlequin can now display
deluded as the universe's fool.

## VII

Deluded as the universe's fool,
and then to think that other worlds suffice,
where gods can madly rant and rave and call
us no more than a random game of dice,

remind me of a Skagen summer day,
when the Meadow Blues as mating birds flew
round like fragmented wisps of clouds all day
and were echoed by Jammerbugten's Blue,

while we who lay there lost among the sand,
as numerous as only two can be,
found our bodies' elements hand in hand

with earth like that between the sea and sky,
two people who to each other bequeath
a life that does not then as nothing die.

## VIII

A life that does not then as nothing die?
What if, in all the works of man, therefore,
in nature's last self-centred upward rise,
we may see ourselves in what's lost before,

may see the least scrap of a loving mind,
of some happiness in a futile act,
as showing us the image of mankind
as grass, though it is the grave's grass in fact.

What use is the great Atlas moth again,
whose wingspan spreads out the world's map today,
looking like memories spun from the brain,

And so we kiss as icons of the dead,
tasting death's kiss which carried them away.
Who has conjured this encounter instead?


## IX

Who has conjured this encounter instead?
It is my brain which is so pale and grey,
that makes light's colours to glow overhead
beyond the butterfly I saw today.

I saw Aurora's pinch of paprika,
its pale gleam of pepper-grey savanna,
and Painted Lady's flight from Africa
straight to winter climes as is its manner.

I saw a Lunar Thorn's outline unfurled,
its tiny, black-bordered moons were crescent,
that sat upon the wingtip of the world.

My vision was not a wild enterprise
imaginings a brain makes up, but blent
with a hint of peace of mind and sweet lies.

**X**

With a hint of peace of mind and sweet lies,
and downy hint of emerald and jade
the Purple Emperor's larvae disguise
themselves resembling willow leaves remade.

I saw them eat their image, self-consumed,
as they folded into a chrysalis,
at last hung up as what it had assumed,
a leaf clustered with other leaves like this.

If by their imagery butterflies
are much more likely to survive by theft
then why should I be any less the wise,

If it will soothe the emptiness and dread
to name the butterflies as souls still left
and summer visions of the vanished dead.


**XI**

And summer visions of the vanished dead,
the Black-veined White that hovers in its flight
like a white cloud with just a hint of red
has flower-traces woven by the light,

Grandmother in the garden's thousandfold
embrace of wallflowers, stocks, bridal wreaths,
and my father who taught me the household
names of all that crawls before its decease,

walk with me into this butterfly vale,
where all that can be is found on this side,
where even the dead hear the nightingale,

its song strikes a strangely sorrowful tone
from not a hint of pain to more beside,
with its deaf rings my ear responds alone.


## XII

With its deaf rings my ear responds alone,
and my eye with its introspective vein,
my heart knows that I am not a no one,
but answers with that well-known stab of pain.

Mirrored in moths of autumns and winters
one evening in November's coppiced oak,
they reflect the shafts of moonlight's splinters
and play at sunshine in the night's dark cloak.

I see them in their pupal torpid sleep,
ruthlessly released in their greatest need
in silvered mirror halls in winter deep,

in the mirror's bare gaze, I realise,
is a lost look and not just death indeed,
death has you in its sights with its own eyes.

### XIII

Death has you in its sights with its own eyes
will see itself in me, who is naive,
as native-born, and so bound up with ties
to stark self-insight in what we call life.

And so I play as on a Wood-White's wing
and fuse phenomena and words alone,
play at being a Fritillary to bring
a myriad of life forms into one.

So I can answer death when it arrives:
I play being a Grayling, dare I hope
I am the face of summer that survives?

I well understand you call me nothing,
but it's me wrapped in an Emperor's cloak,
looking at you from a butterfly's wing.

### XIV

Looking at you from a butterfly's wing,
it feels just like the dust of butterflies,
as fine as nothing and made of nothing,
an answer to the leaves of distant stars,

whirled aloft as light in a summer's wind,
like gleams of mother of pearl, ice and fire,
so all that is when all is left behind
remains itself and is not lost entire,

as Copper, Purple Emperor, Ice Blue
from earth's butterflies it makes a rainbow hue
within earth's own visionary sphere,

a poem the Small Tortoiseshell can bear.
I see dust from the ground begin to rise,
they are rising up, the earth's butterflies.


**XV**
They are rising up, the earth's butterflies
In Brajcino Valley's high noonday heat,
from bitter caverns underground they rise,
hidden in scented mountain brush so sweet.

As Admiral, Camberwell Beauty, Blue,
as Peacock butterflies fluttering by
deluded as the universe's fool
a life that does not then as nothing die.

Who has conjured this meeting instead
with a hint of peace of mind and sweet lies
and summer visions of the vanished dead?

My ear replies to this with its deaf ring:
death has you in its sights with its own eyes
looking at you from a butterfly's wing.

# ELIN AP HYWEL

Translated by Laura Fisk

Elin ap Hywel is one of the most celebrated Welsh-language poets, whose work nevertheless, like that of too many of her fellow country-women and men, has unfortunately remained relatively unknown to English-language readers. She was born in North Wales in 1962 into a Welsh-speaking family and didn't learn to speak English until her family moved to London for a time in the late sixties.

Her poetry explores personal and social themes with a provocative, often ironical lyricism frequently couched in mythological imagery. She is also a highly respected translator of Welsh literature into English, both poetry as well as prose, most notably of much of Menna Elfyn's later work. Menna Elfyn has said of her poetry in Elin's translation that 'these poems became siblings, confident to face the world as proud bilinguals'.

In 2018 Elin was diagnosed with early-onset Alzheimer's.

Photo by Marged Elin Thomas

## Developments

'I don't want to lose you', he said
and set off for Thrace. Therefore
in order to be able to find me again
he left me
in a safe place,
sitting on a stone
on the shore.

He placed a camera in my hands
and said to me
to film him, and the boys, leaving land.

The foam washed
the bottom of my frock, and by the time
his ship was nothing but a comma in the distance
the sea had reached up to my neck
and the film had soaked through.

◆

I have grown a scab
like an old boat that's been
in the harbour too long.
My shoulders are heavy beneath seaweed
and the beams are bowing
with the effort of me trying to remember your name. Oh yes.
I had something to say to you –

Do you see this spider's web that's growing between my legs?
Look! And the moss
embroidering my pubis. Look!
and the goldfish who plays hide-and-seek
through the emptiness of my skull. Look at me, won't you?

Look at me.
Love me.

After all, you made me.


## The Poem's a Gauloise

The poem's a Gauloise –
A stump for us to suck the nicotine of imagination;
smouldering
between the mind's fingers,
by freeing emotions
like a ribbon of blue smoke
turning in the spacious hall of Memory;
before it expires
and is tossed
to the waste paper bin,
to the dusty subconscious

# NILLANTHAN

Translated by Geetha Sukumaran and Shash Trevett

The thirty-year civil war in Sri Lanka came to a devastating end
in May 2009 when thousands of men, women and children were
herded onto a narrow strip of land by the side of Nandikadal lagoon
in Mullivaikkal, and massacred. The UN estimates that between
40,000–70,000 people were killed and thousands still remain
unaccounted for. One of those who survived this atrocity was the
poet Nillanthan, who has written a series of 17 poems charting
the exodus of the people as they were moved from place to place
by the Sri Lankan army.

Nillanthan's poetry, sparse and lacking in sentiment, powerfully
conveys the horrors of war through the lens of food, textiles and the
natural world. He is preoccupied with what people ate, what they
drank, how they cooked food, how they survived. In 'Pina Koorai',
magnificent silk and gold wedding saris are turned into tents,
sleeping mats and sandbags. In 'A Market at the End of an Age' the
price and availability of food at the beginning of the exodus is
compared to what was available at Mullivaikkal where the long march
was to end. These poems are a poetry of witness, yet local culture and
culinary practices are used as screening metaphors with which to
protect the dignity and humanity of those who suffered.

The three poems presented here are the first to be translated into
English as part of Shash's Visible Communities residency at the
National Centre for Writing.

## February 2009

The Mathalan lagoon separates two kingdoms.
Corpses decay in the glutinous Vanni clay.
Even crows do not rest on ancient portia trees.

The school is now a hospital.
On a blackboard, a doctor
keeps score of the injured.

Blood and soil combine in gaping wounds.
Saline hangs from the branches of trees.
Flies swarm on corpses, on shit, on wounds, on dreams.


## Pina Koorai

*The Koorai is the wedding sari, richly embellished with gold patterns.*
*Pina Koorai is the practice of shrouding the body of a dead husband or wife in it.*

The koorai is woven with textured meaning.
Bought after a careful search
it is patterned with joyful memories.
A prized possession kept locked in a box of dreams.

At the end of this age
nothing remains which is sacred.
In three villages, the koorai sari
is now worth less than PP bags.

In a life surrounded by sandbags
where polypropylene is prized above treasure,
we use koorai saris to make sandbags.
We make screens out of them
we spread them on the ground
we wrap ourselves in them
we use them to make roofs.

The koorai make the most beautiful sandbags
but they have lost their meaning,
much like those used to shroud corpses.

Smoke covered the land when Ban Ki-moon
saw these sari-woven death slums
from the air.

Yet the threads of gold glittered
in the sun.

# A Market at the End of an Age

*Valaignar Maddum – Bill of Goods (March - April 2009)*

Anchor milk powder 1Kg – Rs. 2000 - 6000
Rice 1Kg, never less than Rs. 200
Onions 1Kg – Rs. 3000
Dried Chillies 1Kg – Rs. 4000
Lentils 1Kg – Rs. 800
Fish 1Kg – Rs. 2000
Prawns / crabs 1Kg – Rs. 3000
Sugar 1Kg – Rs. 2000
One coconut – Rs. 250 - 350
One betel leaf – Rs. 100
One betel nut – Rs. 200
One t-shirt or shirt – Rs. 500
A saree – Rs. 100-500
One PP Bag – Rs. 50-150
A computer – Rs.1500
One large solar panel – Rs. 5000
One 90amp battery – Rs. 500
An auto rickshaw – Rs. 5000
A motorbike – Rs. 7500
One small mango – Rs. 200
One small candle – Rs. 200
A match box – Rs. 100
One gold sovereign – Rs. 100

*Mullivaikkal – Bill of Goods (May 2009)*

Anchor milk powder 1Kg – Rs. 2000 - 6000

One bar of soap – Rs. 10

Sugar – Rs. 2000

Tamarind – not obtainable.

Unripe tamarind, as a substitute ½ Kilo – Rs. 250

Tamarind leaf, as a further substitute, one handful – Rs.50

Barter an auto rickshaw for a coconut.

Betel leaf – not obtainable.

Instead, substitute with tender coconut-leaf sprouts
or naayunni leaves, one handful – Rs. 50

Betel nut – not obtainable.

Instead substitute with a small unripened coconut – Rs. 20

A baby mango – Rs. 100

A green chilli – Rs. 100

Tender greens, one small bunch – Rs. 200

Clove scented muchuttai leaf, one small bunch – Rs. 100

Ivy gourd leaf, one small bunch – Rs. 100

7 - 8 long beans – Rs. 500

One gold sovereign – Rs. 1000 - 5000.

# NORWID 200

Introduction by Clare Pollard

Cyprian Kamil Norwid is now recognised as one of Poland's greatest
poets, although he was sadly unrecognised in his lifetime, publishing only
one volume which received no critical acclaim. Born 200 years ago near
Warsaw, his life was spent as an outsider – much of it in poverty and exile,
suffering from TB and increasing deafness. Norwid died in Paris, in a
shelter for impoverished Polish war veterans and orphans, in 1883.
Despite this, he managed to produce an abundance of art, as a poet,
novelist, playwright, sculptor, painter and draughtsman, all of which is
notable for its striking empathy. In C. K. Norwid, *Poems*, translated by
Danuta Borchardt, his famous poem 'Larva' begins by noticing the
outcast on the street:

> On slippery London pavement
> In fog, sub-lunar, white –
> Many a creature will pass by,
> You'll remember her, terrified.

'To Citizen John Brown' – written for the abolitionist, who was hung
for inciting a slave insurrection – begins with a gesture of solidarity
and connection with the criminalised and oppressed: 'Over the Ocean's
undulant plain | A song, like a *seagull*, I send you, o! John...'
   We are proud to be working with the Polish Cultural Institute to
commemorate Norwid 200 years after his birth, and help bring his legacy
to the wider attention of an English-speaking audience. We present here a
fine translation of his poem 'The Last Despotism' by Adam Czerniawski,
along with two newly commissioned responses to Norwid's poetry by
UK poets Malika Booker and Wayne Holloway-Smith. We will also be
publishing, online, a sparkling translation of Norwid's verse comedy of
manners *Pure Love at Sea-Side Bathing* by Adam Czerniawski, unperformed
in Norwid's lifetime, with new animations by Emma Brierley: Temporary
Commons, produced in partnership with Golden Hour Productions.

# CYPRIAN KAMIL NORWID

Translated by Adam Czerniawski

## The Last Despotism

'What news?' – 'Despotism's abolished!... I have it all:
And here's the dispatch...'

             'I trust you are well –
Be seated – dispatch... it says?... Do take a chair!
But wait – I hear a mackintosh swishing in the hall –
Someone's coming! – It's the Baron – recovered from his fall...
Please sit! – What news can the Baron share...'

             ◆

'And that dispatch... it says what...? A sugared drink?
Or perhaps an orange?...' 'In Greece –
Locusts – on Cyprus a village slipped over the brink –
Adelina Patti's singing in 'The Golden Fleece' –
I see the orange's from Malta – it's very sweet.'
'Have another...'

             ◆

    '...and how is Despotism in defeat??'

             ◆

But they've just announced the ex-chamberlain's wife
And her adopted son – 'What's your view of nepotism?
The boy's older than his mother by a year and a head...
Here they are...'
    '...and now, this Despotism – is it dead?...'

# MALIKA BOOKER

Over the ocean's undulant plain
A song, like a *seagull*, I send you, o! John...

Reading Polish poet Cyprian Kamil Norwid's poem *To Citizen John Brown* written in November 1858, I am struck by his empathy and compassion for the abolitionist John Brown's cause balanced with harsh criticism levied against America's brutal institution of slavery. It was profound reading this elegiac critique against the backdrop of an international community gripped with the dramatic tension of George Floyd's trial, and still witnessing daily public lynching of Black bodies at the hands of the American police.

I was struck by the small exhalations of breath resonant throughout the poem, in its dramatic exclamations of the vowel o! and its echoes throughout the poem: *over | ocean | John | on | for | gone | rope | your | stone | fold | douse | crown |* - Here the vowel o! becomes litany and most importantly reverberates in many ways with song. Yet is reminiscence of a tiny gut wrenched sigh – which takes on massive contemporary resonance read against a litany of witnesses in a court of law repeating the circumstances surrounding George Floyd's last breath.

This o! bears the qualities of testimony, solace, and healing evocative of negro spirituals, and Mahalia Jackson and Aretha Franklin's gospels. Each defiant couplet is melody – ageless hymn resilient, yet radical. The o! alongside the quiet power of dashes and eclipses demonstrate the horrors language is too inadequate to capture and I wanted my poetic response to answer the o! this mouth round in protest, this vessel for sound, and this moan from the fragile throat.

## To Poet Cyprian Kamil Norwid

*(From a letter written to America in 2021, in April)*

Cyprian (Polish brethren poet from our past)
can I tell you there is a heft to your o!
A whole poem in the exclamation o! Here
a mouth is tunnel for change. The mouth
a vessel, this o! with implicit no and groan,
hummed from the backs of throats, sounding
like rope. The rope which would swing
black men like unlit lanterns in the Southern prison
of night where white men hunted after twilight.
Freedom's noose bloomed bruised blues
in your, *night coming – a black night with a black*
*face!* I too write a letter to America, asking
how *the land of the free maybe in vain,* asking
definition between lynched and hanged? Asking
o! This poem is also song, and dirge, asking
a repeated chorus o! Humming the gospels
of the South, as Aretha Franklin and Mahalia
Jackson's throats pelt out soulful melodies,
grievance sore and John Brown's soul does not go
marching on. It is April and there is still no *old*
*John Brown,* no *Glory, Glory, Hallelujah.* There is no
spring, only cold sleet as I too write a letter to America.
o! Cyprian now men die in chokeholds and fluttering
breath has replaced the fluttering feet of the hanged,
muttering *I can't breathe,* breath flailing
like the beheaded chicken flapping into death.
Cyprian, know we held our breath at George's
trial as four more died between lawyer's summary
and verdict and know that these too are spectacle,
now the noose is a knee on the back of a throat.

# WAYNE HOLLOWAY-SMITH

At the time I received this commission, I'd been rereading Roland Barthes' *Camera Lucida*, in which he describes the unexpected 'something' of a photograph, a latent aspect, which triggers a response after the viewing. He says, 'to see a photograph well, it is best to close your eyes or look away.' This is how I approached the life and work of Norwid. I read everything I had been sent, then looked away. After understanding the primary concerns and politics, I closed my eyes. Sometime later, the 'something' which continued to move me was the empathy rolled out through everything I had experienced.

For me, then, the poem I ended up making isn't a one-for-one trade off with a specific aspect of Norwid, but takes inspiration from that sense of empathy I'd found. Beginning with the opening lines of Norwid's poem 'To Citizen John Brown', then combed through with the understanding of the life of the poet – the idea that someone suffering is also able to reach out of that suffering to someone else, in a gesture of compassion. Being able to offer nourishment from the distant location of that suffering, struck me heavily. The London in 'Larva' me made want to contemporise its streets – which the Deliveroo driver (the 'he' sent by the 'I') is navigating in order to get to the 'you'. The gesture from me isn't as big as the original poem's intention. And perhaps doesn't lean heavily into its politics. But, like Barthes suggests, what succeeds the artist, after he has left us or after we have left him, has a strength and currency of its own. It provides us something invigorating to love with and aspire to. Here, for me, that is empathy.

## Rabbits

I am sending you a sandwich from deep under my sadness
the man in his clean-shaved legs is coming
unharmed with breathable synthetics a happy little bag
he is weaving by uneven roads and cranes and circular-blue
lights are ululating in my room my abdomen thumping
I-love-you-so-much-cardiovascular lactic acids pending
his knees his thighs are calling upon glucose he is breathing
torn and rebirthed muscle I want you to know
the past is speeding away his kidneys are doing their best
I want you to know the blood vessels in his skin are dilating red
and burned with o god you are my favourite when he arrives

# ROMALYN ANTE

Translated by Romalyn Ante

Tagalog, like many other languages, can be challenging to translate into English. It is because there are words that are just untranslatable, and some of our ways of constructing a sentence, especially with regards to the verb-pronoun relationship, can be different from that of English construction.

In my original poem, there is a line that says 'dampa ng pangako at pagbibiro', literally 'hut of promises and jokes'. But I translated 'pagbibiro' (jokes) as 'pretence' because I wanted to include a sense of mischief that fits with the poem's theme. In the poem, 'pagbibiro' cannot be merely an act of 'joking' or 'bantering', it must also signify a behaviour that is associated in young, unserious love and must contain a sense of mischief in it. So I use the word 'pretence'.

Tagalog verbs can be quite porous and ephemeral. Even though we have simple past, present, and future tenses like the English language, some of our verbs can stay in the present participle but still denote that the actions have already happened, i.e. the line 'where you ground the coffee beans' has an original transliteration of 'where you *grinding* the coffee beans'. We do not change the verb 'to be', we do not go from 'is' to 'was', thus we do not have a past continuous tense. Instead, we measure time using other devices. But to achieve more clarity in English, I used the simple past tense for this.

# Forgetting

And even if you curse the volcano in the north
I will still not remember your face.
And even if you gather all the stars thrown away
by the rebellious clouds of yesterday,
I will still not be able to trace the scent
of the kapeng barako you boil
on the rusty stove at twilight.
Your gaze is always on the horizon, coaxing
the sky the colour of purple yam and java apple,
waiting for the paper that will take you
to the other town crammed with glimmer.

Don't you know? I have forgotten you too –
and there, in the hut of promises and pretence,
where I let the wind steal
my embroidered handkerchief, I have realised
the difference between kindness and love.
I have burnt all the guava leaves
that once scraped the fragrance of your voice.
And the bench in the shade of kamatchile
where you ground the coffee beans
is now rotting. Only bird and hen droppings
can make the brittle bamboo sparkle.

# ENDRE RUSET

Translated by Harry Man

In 2014, I met Endre Ruset on a bus while travelling through Matka Canyon in what is now called North Macedonia. At the time, *Elsket og savnet* (Loved and Missed) his collection of short elegies, had just come out with Kolon Publishing. He described an attentive and severe editing process, using the conceit of a 'house' as both a literal and figurative container of grief. The house becomes a place where the boundary between the state of inner grief and the world dissolve. 'She draws lightning | and the lightning turns to fire | and the fire spreads with the wind'. There are traces of Gunvor Hofmo and Tor Ulven, two key twentieth century figures in Norwegian poetry who dealt respectively with the psychological trauma of World War II and less of a psychogeography and more of a psycho-geology, where the strata in a rockface become accumulated thoughts that 'you are thinking about, in darkness | the white flowers, | that we are dust'.

On July 22nd 2011 a lone-wolf terrorist detonated a bomb in Regjeringskvartalet, outside the headquarters of the Norwegian Labour Party in downtown Oslo. He then drove 24 miles north to a summer camp on the island of Utøya where he killed an additional 69 people, most of them teenagers. The youngest was just 14.

For the past four years, Endre Ruset and I have been working on a long seventy-poem sequence of concrete elegies to commemorate those who died. These poems are from that sequence.

The Brothers
Lionheart leapt to be
yond their deaths, on to Nangi
jala and Nangilima. Alice fell
down into a                         new story,
through a                              secret
hole in the                            ground.
Inside the                             ward
robe,                                  Lucy
stum                                   bled
             into           the    snow
                                       in a
forest.                                But no
other ma                               teriality
begins once                            you dis
appear.            Foot        prints
finish loose, in                  mid-air;
a blind spot on                   *Kjær*
*lighetsstien.* A new blind       spot in the
eye. A point in the middle        of the world.
A point without a point.

In a drenched pullover. Trying.
To lie still. Flecks of rain dew a
crushed mobile screen, crushed glass
es. We hide behind a rock. The three
of us. Hearing horses. We hear horses–the
horses scr                         eaming through
the rain,                             the wood,
with                                    heads, manes,
flanks                                  someone has
set fire to.                                    The horses
burn.        All          on fire.    All a
                                                 fl
                                              ame.


            Horses


                                               pound
            ing.                      Each burning
      to the ground.              Trying to consider
    whether to breathe. To r      un. To stay down. To run.
Just run. When we can hear  nothing but the sway of the trees
in the rain. The three of us. Hiding behind a
rock. Try to lie still.

You stand
beneath and outside it
what must be your face rising
to your face in the morning and setting
in the evening. When          the face
disappears.                        The dark
draws in.                          At night,
dreaming.                          I am
under a diff                       erent light.
A face on      its      arc        through the
heavens. The                       heavens are a root
cellar. Across the                 attic floor sparrows
lie strewn, they glow,             each one more pin-hole
bright than the sun.     A wing    shrinks to a feather.
A feather is drawn into            the wind – a first.
The horizon is brief               and dispiriting.
The missing lie                    strewn like dead sparrows
on the attic floor.                Absent-minded, I fall
upon your face in dreams.          Your face is a hole that emits
light. Grief is a clock. Invisible complete. Not me.

I don't want
to remember which
stones in the garden you
loved to tip up. To watch the
woodlice run in every direction. Or
fall, get back up and stumble away. I don't
want to remember your rain boots under the
deck. The                stripes of light catching
the                          cobwebs around them
like                             hidden treasure.
You                                   could do anything
better,                              than
any          one
I


knew.
More          hero than          human.
Fun                          even
through the                   cracks of
lightning that                 made the pair of us freeze.
I don't want to remember          so many of the things that make
me turn to the amber glass of          one of our cereal bowls. The kind
you'd eat your cornflakes from every day. The kind I carried into the road,
when I heard the news and smashed against the asphalt. I don't want to
think of your face. It shines too fiercely back at me. Through me. The glass
remains shattered, bright, like a firework pinned to a permanent night.

# THREE ISTRIAN POETS

Translated by André Naffis-Sahely

If current trends continue unabated, Istrian literature may soon be the sole repository of the beauties of Istriot, an indigenous Western Romance language once widely used across south-western Istria and now spoken by fewer than a thousand people in a handful of small villages along the northern Croatian coast. Classified by UNESCO as 'severely endangered', Istriot shares affinities with Croatian, Venetian and German, exemplifying how the land rapidly changed hands between the Venetian Empire, Austria-Hungary, Fascist Italy, Yugoslavia and now Croatia in only slightly over two centuries. Often seen as an anachronistic rural dialect generally spoken by the old, Istriot is not taught in schools today and its future therefore appears very uncertain.

The poets featured in this selection are Ligio Zanini (1927–1993), whom Claudio Magris once called the greatest Istriot poet of the 20th century, as well as the contemporary voices Lidia Delton (1951–) and Loredana Bogliùn (1955–). Istriot's status as the so-called 'dialect' of an embattled minority finds no better expression than in Zanini's poem 'Sensa nom' or 'Without a Name'. A riddle of sorts, the speaker in 'Sensa nom' is actually a whitebait, the tiny fish that inhabit the Adriatic waters of the poet's beloved Istria. When the speaker in the poem says 'we were many without a name | they scooped us up by the thousands | but we were many all the same', Zanini here also refers to the enormous exodus of Istrians prompted by Yugoslavia's annexation of the region in the wake of World War II and the cultural devastation that accompanied it.

## LIGIO ZANINI

Translated by André Naffis-Sahely

### Without a Name

We were many without a name,
they scooped us up by the thousands
but we were many all the same.

Only a nameless few remain,
few of us get scooped up now and
fewer still grow old in our domain.

You poison our eggs with your pollution
and for us few in our native seas,
death is but a foregone conclusion.

We the nameless are not to blame,
we had no teeth with which to bite,
all you'll need will be your eyes to cry
because you killed us out of spite.


## LIDIA DELTON

Translated by André Naffis-Sahely

### An Old Photograph

How many times did we
glance at it together
and how you never tired
of telling me:
grandma Matiusa,
auntie Macaca,
my brother Nane,

grandpa Zanito when he was a soldier,
but if only you knew
how to me
they all looked alike
because nobody
wears those clothes anymore
those chignon buns
aren't fashionable any longer,
instead of grandpa's leggings
people now wear socks.
Now
I look at these photographs again
and concentrate
and force myself to recognize
grandma, auntie, your brother.
my grandfather
and I cry
and I can no longer hear
your voice
how it would patiently
explain it all to me,
once, twice, a hundred times.
Ah, if only I'd listened...


**LOREDANA BOGLIÙN**

Translated by André Naffis-Sahely

## A Touch of Boùmbaro

A touch of Boùmbaro
how jotting down even a couple of lines
for this land can be so special
until one can talk about

the stairs that collapsed
or that door that hasn't been there
in who knows how long. And the grass darkens
– the rain makes it grow –
it makes no sense to speak of yesterday.
Today the old have forgotten this tongue.
I'd love for them to listen to me
so I could tell them a few things. That it's beautiful.
My son, in his misfortune,
will never learn it,
nonetheless he will inherit
a touch of Boùmbaro from his mother
because I'll teach him how to pick asparagus,
or how to keep an eye out for snakes.
His grandfather will take him
out in his cart along with the donkeys in their stall
to show him where the border with Lacòusso lies.
He'll understand this land from within.
You must speak to your own children
so that these people of tomorrow
will have something to talk about.
They too must never forget that in the past
living was a struggle and how
in the evening, farmers were dead tired
having worked like dogs
for a morsel of bread.

# JACQUES BREL

Translated by Paul Roddie

In the course of translating Jacques Brel's 'Amsterdam' into English, it soon became clear that the translation had to be more than a transposition from one language to another, and that it had to exist as a poem in English in its own right. In order to do so, I have respected the rhyme schemes of the original while remaining scrupulously faithful to its meaning. The two well-known translations of the poem in English are unfortunately riddled with mistakes, often of an elementary nature, and images which do not exist in the original. Embroidering the text in unnecessary ways, I feel they fail to do justice to Brel's words.

To recreate the prosody of the original, I have used syllabic verse with alternating lines of seven syllables ('they rise with a booming laugh' | 'for boozy woozy sailors') and six syllables ('and they rub as they prance' | 'How they reel, how they spin'). These variations afforded me the latitude to avoid syntactic contortions and forced rhymes. I have also drawn on alliteration wherever possible in order to enrich the musical qualities of the text.

One idiom which was particularly difficult to translate was 'A décroisser la lune' which is a neologism and translates roughly as 'to un-crescent' or 'to de-crescent' the moon. However, whereas this transposition from noun to verb is perfectly plausible in French, it felt laboured in English and I found it necessary to reshape the whole line as a result.

I hope to have rendered the Brueghelian qualities and carnival-like atmosphere of Jacques Brel's poem with verve and a touch of humour while making it both entertaining and enjoyable for an English reader.

# Amsterdam

In the port of Amsterdam
there are sailors who chant
of strange dreams which enchant
on the waves off Amsterdam

In the port of Amsterdam
all along the sullen quays
you can see the sailors laze
like the drooping oriflammes

In the port of Amsterdam
as the light of dawn hovers
the old sea dogs keel over
from the night's drunken drama

In the port of Amsterdam
they then rise from the dead
in the air heavy as lead
which the high seas embalm

In the port of Amsterdam
watch them stuffing their chops
at the whitest table-tops
where fish squirm in greasy palms

Rows of pearly whites they bare
that could maul the hand of fate
warp the lone moon's crescent shape
gnaw the shrouds till they're threadbare

And all around the foul stench
of whoring by every wench
while the men with podgy mitts
bid for more fish and chips

Then once they've had enough
they rise with a booming laugh
and hoist their zips back up
bowing out with a burp

In the port of Amsterdam
the mariners they all dance
and they rub as they prance
their paunches against the dames

How they reel, how they spin
like suns spat out of the sky
to the mournful melody
of the wheezing accordion

Craning their necks to hear
their shipmates' hearty cheer
till shrilly above the laughs
the accordion breathes its last

Then, with countenance profound
their faces proud and bold
they whip their manhood out
for all present to behold

In the port of Amsterdam
there's always rum galore
for boozy, woozy sailors
to knock back dram by dram

As they toast the charms so fair
of the whores of Amsterdam
of Hamburg and God knows where –
the finest dames in the land

Who flog their dainty wares
and sell their virtue short
for a few measly guilders
to the sozzled old stalwarts

Who cock their snouts at the spheres
then blow their snot at the stars
spray piss while I shed tears
o'er the troths of flighty tarts

in the port of Amsterdam
in the port of Amsterdam

Auteur-compositeur: Jacques Brel.

# JEAN-CLAUDE AWONO

Translated by Georgina Collins

Awono's poetry is striking for the way it makes language so physical, not just in his use of words, but in the way language and all its facets become characters in many of his poems. This is particularly pronounced in 'To Get Through the Night', where verbs and pronouns play a tangible role in expressing the futility of language in the face of corporal brutality.

The poem was written in French originally, but also uses words from Camfranglais and Pidgin. This focus on language is apt, for in Cameroon today, issues of language are highly debated and politically sensitive due to the present conflict between Anglophone separatists and central government (based in Yaounde, in the Francophone Central Region). Alongside English and French, the country's two official languages, hundreds of African languages are also spoken. Awono uses local language to firmly locate the text in Cameroon, and this been retained in the translation to keep the cultural and political resonances of the poem.

Awono is a performance poet and the sounds of spoken words, including strong plosive consonants throughout, were embraced in translation because of this. These sounds, along with the use of alliteration, assonance and consonance are also manifest in 'Tomorrow will be Beautiful like Death'. This poem too has political significance, and having a cultural understanding of the country is helpful to the translation. Through Awono's words, and those of the translation, we can picture the fighting and loss of lives in Cameroon's war-torn North West and South West regions and battles against Boko Haram in the Far North. However, this poem has a wider reverberation and can be read in relation to more global political threats.

Words are the nonsense of nutters' inanity
When I was crawling
They didn't help me
They didn't see my broken body
They didn't save me
From my hangover oozing with slaver
They stopped me
They caged me
They beat me
They slaughtered me
And nothing was said
They were only able to aim their ignorant eyes
At the tele
At the blue-light display
The pleasure of the page
Words are the sapaks of sotucs in the brothels of imboucs
They were there when they hanged me
When the straw broke the camel's back
And my buttocks stifled the shit
Not a verb nor a pronoun lifted a finger
To index my executioners
Not a sentence has roared with rage
To magnify my misery
Not a comma on the corner of my night
Not a vuvuzela to play out my pain
Nor a minguili tom-tom to declare my death
And now I'll place all my faith
In the dregs

I'll pick myself up and surrender to the scum
You, Silence come come and kiss me darling
You, at least you came and gave me a bottle
**To get through the night**


Slogans wave their flags
Impotence raises its head
Each patch of life erases what is possible
Dreaming is desperate
All power lies in departing
And throwing towards the borders
And sending into war
Troops of children
Exile and death
Will be the country of tomorrow
Tomorrow will be beautiful like death
And red like blood
And clean like pus
**Tomorrow will be beautiful like death**
And spilt upon smoking sand
Departing swindles the triangle
And slogans flutter
Like flies
On the streets of the Republic

# IF NO ONE NAMES US

*Focus on Mexico*

# NAHUI OLIN

Translated by Claire Mullen

Nahui Olin (born Carmen Mondragón, 1893) was a poet, painter, and artist's model active in Mexico City in the 1920s and 30s. She posed for artists including Diego Rivera, Edward Weston, and Jean Charlot, and often painted colourful scenes of herself with her lovers. She was widely known for her large green eyes and fiery spirit, which were speculated upon in social columns of the time. As Mexico's social and political spheres swung more conservative in the 1940s, Olin distanced herself from public life, but she continued to teach art to children in Mexico City schools for decades, until her death in 1978.

The poems 'Insatiable Thirst' and 'Enormous Mountain' were written in the early 1920s, and are included in Olin's first poetry collection, Óptica cerebral: poesía dinámica. The book consists of 27 poems that codify Olin's thoughts on the significance of scientific discoveries of her time – Einstein's theory of general relativity, the discovery of black holes, and theories of colour and optics – alongside discussions of sexuality, feminism, and Mexican nationality. The book was illustrated by Dr. Atl, a writer, painter, and volcanologist, and Olin's lover at the time.

Although Olin has largely been remembered as a muse and model, there has been a recent resurgence of interest in her own work after a re-release of a biography by journalist Adriana Malvido, and a retrospective of her paintings at the Museo Nacional de Arte. Olin's books are currently out of print in Spanish, however Dr. Patricia Rosas Lopategui has published a selection in her book Nahui Olin: Sin principio ni fin, where these poems were found.

## Insatiable Thirst

My spirit and my body are forever mad with thirst
for those new worlds
that I go on endlessly creating,
and of the things
and of the elements,
and of the beings,
that enter ever new phases
under the influence
of my spirit and my body eternally mad with
thirst;
unquenchable thirst, a creative restlessness,
which toys with the new worlds
that I go on endlessly creating
and with the things that are one, and that are many.
And with the elements,
and with the beings
that give me insatiable thirst –
and I don't know
if they have
A bit of blood –
Or a bit of flesh
Or a bit of spirit –
That serves as fitful games to the sensibility
Of my subject.
And my spirit is forever mad with thirst –
Truly wild thirst
For itself –
To create
To possess

And destroy alongside a creation of greater magnitude, and my spirit
    has a wild thirst
that will never be extinguished, because its singular charm will never
    allow communion
or possession of equal magnitude.
And in vain,
In those new worlds
That I am endlessly creating,
In the things
In the elements
In the beings, sensuously imbuing surfaces with appreciative caresses,
    it penetrates
them, shovels them into its fleshiness and bites down to drink their
    blood without
achieving anything more than a tremendous curse of insatiable thirst.
And from that admirable thirst creative power is born –
And my body does not resist the fire, which in continuous renewal of
    the flesh of youth
and of spirit is one and is all, an insatiable thirst.
My spirit and my body are forever mad with thirst...

## The Enormous Mountain That Has At Its Peak a Tomb, Time

Time is a massive mountain, which has at its peak a tomb, mysterious and profound. It opens its mouth of wide sensual lips, and coldly buries in its terrifying chaos of oblivion and silence, to generations of physical beauty, it absorbs matter with the precision of a destructive machine, it is ruthless with the invigorating magnetism of inspiring loveliness, and with a voracious appetite crushes things of irreplaceable beauty –

Time in unconscious evolution destroys and propagates wonders, and in its multiple powers of regeneration and destruction, purifies what is between its claws, and in maximum superlative creates each time a world superior to the one that now mummifies in the tomb on top of the massive mountain.–

In a futurism fever it aims for the inconceivable, and makes worlds of the human hearts crushed by its tremendous mouth of wide, sensual lips.–

Only in the face of enduring cerebral strength did it close its mouth, leaving the eternal world behind.–

It is the cold conclusion of what stays and what goes.–

# NATALIA TOLEDO

Translated by Clare Sullivan and Irma Pineda

*Modern Poetry in Translation*'s issue *The Tangled Route* (2015, no. 3) included poems from Natalia Toledo's award-winning collection *Guie' yaase'* (The Black Flower). These three poems come from her latest anthology, *Deche biotope* (The Crab's Hard Shell). Natalia Toledo's bilingual poetry (Zapotec-Spanish) provides an important voice for the often-overlooked but vast and rich tradition of indigenous poetry in Mexico. She translated her own poems into Spanish and her fellow poet Irma Pineda helped me to translate them into English.

This kind of community effort is required to capture the subtleties in verses that merge different cultures. In 'The Visitor', for example, Pineda explained the belief that a turtle's tears when giving birth are a farewell to her young. The 'one tree' in 'Family' is the

pochote: not only the one that stands at the center of her village providing shade for games and story-telling and seed pods to stuff mattresses, but also the tree at the center of the Zapotec universe whose roots formed the first humans. 'The Zapotec' means literally 'the people of the clouds' and that poem is a litany to Toledo's region and its customs. But these poems also expose her own pain and that of her people in images at once elegant and raw. Like the crab, she edges into the past, but the hard shell of experience or cynicism provides only temporary protection for the human vulnerability beneath it.

## Visitor

He appears beneath the olive flower
and pricks the moon's navel.
You cry like a turtle each time she lays eggs:
she knows she'll never see her children again.
You roll up in the woven corners of your petate,
ants pinch your body.
Before the wind bends your back,
stretch out a hammock of stars and
release the threads that tangle you.

## Family

*For Henrik Nordbrandt*

Since they're shrimp,
some have buried their heads in mud.
Me, I'd much rather go round and round the tree –
that one tree – with my basket,
each leaf was a fish that talked to me
beneath the scales of the sun.
The grackle's song is the sickle of the waning moon.
We all have family,
just as we all have styes in our eyes
that ache and make us cry.


## The Zapotec

I search the distant clouds
for our ancestors' writing.
I love the otters' rivers,
the isthmus and its sinkholes,
the sea's lips and her saltiness,
her umbilical cord and her tombs of broken gourds
that drag beneath the earth.
We have roots in the clouds,
but they are faithful to the wind.

# PITA AMOR

Translated by Amanda Hopkinson and Nick Caistor

Pita Amor was born Guadalupe Teresa Amor Schmidtlein in Mexico City in 1918, the youngest of seven children of mixed French, German and Spanish ancestry. The family belonged to the Euro-Mexican aristocracy, and were stripped of their considerable wealth by the Mexican Revolution (1910–20). Loss and nostalgia characterise *Yo soy mi Casa* (I Am my Home, 1946), dedicated to her close friend Gabriela Mistral, the great Chilean poet and Latin America's first Nobel prizewinner.

This first of her 25+ volumes of poetry was so innovatory that Amor became known as 'the 11th Muse of Mexico'. The 10th muse was the 17th-century nun, Sor Juana Inés de la Cruz, whose *décimas* (10-line 'sonnets'), were as much a springboard for Amor's own *Décimas a Dios* (Poems to God), as the Baroque excesses of the similarly metaphysical Spanish nobleman, Francisco de Quevedo.

Amor's poetry plundered her own frequently tormented life, with an audacity and assurance very much of her own time. A dancer, actress and artist's model, she arrived at sittings for Diego Rivera or Juan Soriano nude beneath her mink coat. Her largely Bohemian circle extended to Picasso and visiting Surrealists, as well as close friends, Frida Kahlo and film star María Félix; writers Elena Garro, Juan Rulfo, and her early mentor, the poet and philosopher Alfonso Reyes.

Sadly, her notoriety outlasted her writing career. In 1943, her only child died in a drowning accident, aged 18. Although Amor continued writing, it was with increasing difficulty, and her fame waned. She died in Mexico City in 2000, years after Michael K. Schuessler's biography (*Guadalupe Amor: La Undécima Musa*) was published, awakening renewed interest in Mexico's 'Eleventh Muse'. I am indebted to her niece, author Elena Poniatowska, for championing and introducing me to her poetry.

## Jet Black Mourning

Jet black mourning weeds
a crow's dark wings in flight
through past skies it speeds
soon passing out of sight
down corridors of night.

## From *My House was Round*

I

My house was round
by solitude surrounded:
the air swept around
murmuring a rounded harmony
breathless anxiety abounded.

Morning transformed into night,
nights that vanished,
sorrows to be celebrated,
and joys to be banished.

And from this rounded world,
by absence surrounded,
my heart emerged wounded
my soul deeply troubled.
One memory imprinted:
the surrounding nothing redoubled.

## II

Ladders lacking rungs
bring only sorrows to me,
chains of disillusion,
I offer the world for free.

They take different forms
and assume another shape,
yet united down the years,
my sorrows and my fears,
a pearl necklace of my tears,
an inner ladder make.

## III

From my spherical notion of things,
emerge my disquiet, my curiosity,
since, geometrically, to me
large and small are equal, by being
equal in importance: simply by existing,
their size has no dimension,
their dimensions lack proportion,
all that now counts is their completion,
however, forever unequal their sphere.

## IV

I'm turning towards the outside, here
I'm drowning deep inside my mind.
The world is no more than a sphere
and from the world I need to hear,
of the totality I cannot find.

A totality I should fashion,
within myself create,
by striving to negate
all my piteous passion;
in order now to delete
my overweening pride
and thus would I distinguish
the way to make my soul complete.

V

From my baroque brain,
my soul emerges intact;
while my body exacts
revenge against them both.

All my being in quest
of an end it cannot reach:
my soul slips between each
letting both be free
on either land or sea
held in an embrace.

## VI

Concave and convex am I;
two half-worlds at the same time:
the wildness I show outside,
and the one entirely mine.
They compose two curves divided
authentically in me combined,
in heights and depths united
in my essence there refined.

Thus, do I learn, exist
black merging to white as well,
and as tortuously persist
mingling heaven and hell.

# JUANA ADCOCK

Translated by Robin Myers

These two poems come from Juana Adcock's collection *Manca*.
Dense, rich, and often darkly funny, this book examines the experi-
ence of registering horror from afar. Adcock grew up in the northern
Mexican state of Nuevo León, which was ravaged by narco-violence
from 2009 and 2013. At that point, she was already living in Scotland,
and she has described her writing process as an experience of engag-
ing with this crisis without being there to witness it. *Manca* contains
poems that shatter and kaleidoscopically reassemble into new forms
of mourning, mockery, protest, exultation, storytelling, and laughter.
It explores the impact of violence not only on human bodies and
communities, but also on the language used to understand – or
manipulated to suppress – shared experience.

Adcock's poems are both thrilling and daunting to translate.
Some are already bilingual works in themselves: she wrote them not
in Spanish but in Spanglish, which raises important questions about
the different kinds of work – aesthetic and invariably political – being
done by both Spanish and English. Other poems, like 'The Body of a
Woman I Inhabit' and 'Parrot', involve what I came to think of as
sonic and syntactic graftings. In every sense, it was among the most
gratifyingly collaborative translation experiences I've had. I learned
so much from Juana's own responses and suggestions – as well as her
encouragement to focus as much on sound, on the sheer material
experience of language, as on anything else.

## This Body of a Woman I Inhabit

This body of a woman I inhabit
from which I've raised a hand to touch the hair on the head of a
Moses suddenly moved
to the inside-out weeping of an entire childhood
of slicing rabbits upper lip stiffened bearing the world
having his way with voltmeters brandishing monkey wrenches
drilling walls soldiers protecting
the softness of our angles our wisdom of curtains, from which I've
batted eyelashes to seduce three, four from which I've traced
the sinuous *s* of desire
which Cratylus called 'serpent' and Adam called 'perception of flux'
from which I've tired of nursing
        like Teresa and Diana
the fear they didn't feel when they touched lepers
with their immaculate hands, the lips
with which they kissed
their blessed wounds, from which I've scrubbed the axel grease
letting fibers soak in a universal river of saliva from which I've bled
drops miscarried fertilized the wheat the ivy from which I've been
all-fat of the land where goats graze

## Parrot

Paydirt parrot the gilt of time notintime that part of Monterrey
soslumber that ship dividing time the ashtrees the frescos the
evenings the longedfor blush the tithing

A woman green purple yellow scratched lashed feet bound and
message carved into soles, it was just a pair of blue pants shirtless
headless splintered nipples sick kids at least we got out early but fuck
they really went too far

We got up and the city wet behind the glass smoked with perfumes
neighborhood geraniums cypress and thyme

The mutilated bodies walk past with their umbrellas their raincoats
their ironclad crystalline containers

Not a head, not a good idea, but a body? sure why not

Burn! Burn till you vanish! it said to the head

And the head turned in the hearth and spoke when we couldn't cut
the skin that divided us where we exposed our principles were beset
by exhaustions the little ones trauma clingings overwhelmedness
rejections when time ran a ramshackle machine or the turtledove
caged in the chest whose terrified

Sleeping cadaver

Didn't take us running round the world parroting 'mandala,
archpriest, midwife, isotope, razzle-dazz'

# GUILLERMO FERNÁNDEZ

Translated by Adriana Diaz-Enciso

In the enigmatic images of this poem there is a poignant tenderness, a call for some transcendent protection that yet doesn't have the power to deliver from sorrow. It is, as other poems by Guillermo Fernández, a prayer. Though Fernández was a caustic critic of the shortcomings of organised religion, he created through poetry a religion of his own, a language to articulate the need to salvage things obscurely felt as sacred from the helplessness of the human condition and its burden of grief and loss, often perturbed by the wild beasts of love and desire.

Whose is the voice pleading with the holy mother figure to protect her child, referred to in the third person? Aware of the sublime care the mother is capable of as much as of the brokenness of the child who grew into life and its bitter lessons, it holds in its omniscience both the supplication and the fall. This conjunction of mystery and raw humanity, the seemingly mother and Christ figures devoid of dogma yet imbued with the holiness of compassion and sorrow, and the delicate beauty of the images make of this one of my favourite poems by Guillermo.

As one of the foremost translators of Italian literature in Latin America, he knew that the perfect translation is an impossibility. Though I accept, as he did, the defeat beforehand, I hope I've managed to convey in this version the subtle and complicated power of his poem.

In 2012, Fernandez was found dead at his home. The coward hand of Guillermo's still unknown murderer will never succeed in silencing his voice.

## Dark-skinned Hand on a White Tablecloth

Lady,
lull your little one,
in your powerful hands hush him to sleep.
There is a small fold for him
in the cloak that shelters the Earth,
a caress of your protective hand.
He wanted to live among men,
to rouse in his blood the dominion of light
in a pale and icy world,
to alleviate the burden of grave love.
Far from you,
he learnt with his first steps
that the dead under the earth
talk about things less sad than us;
that he who lives for dreaming only
becomes a walking dream.
Reality poured out its acids
upon his awkward heart,
thirty-three peals stunned him;
he found that the closest things
lay their being on the horizon when touched by hatred
and the fair graceful monster.
Protect the scales around his heart,
may that parched wind graze them no more.
Take him high up in the Valley,
tell him of the blue bee of childhood,
of the dark-skinned hand on the white tablecloth,
of the fruit caressed in silence,
of the oil lamp herald of your arrival

like a feeble dawn birthing in your bosom
– when you caught him
stumbling on the shadow at every step,
invoking protection amidst his tears
and you comforted him:
'Don't be afraid, my love, it's just the wind'
knowing that his ship foundered
in the deep stare of the night.
The truth in his eyes is yours at last.
He's tired
and wishes to live nowhere but in the shade of your gaze.
Cradle him in your womb,
lessen him in the neatness of a white leaf,
in the silt of the gods' first thought.
The colour of another gaze deepens in his eyes,
dark like a beauteous melancholy.
The blossom of three summers toppled down.
The legend ends as your child goes back home.
May he sleep in your lap
and find his peace at last.

# MIKEAS SÁNCHEZ

Translated by Wendy Call

Mikeas Sánchez writes in her native Zoque, an indigenous language spoken in southern Mexico. In translating this series of twelve poems, I relied primarily on Mikeas Sánchez's Spanish versions. I studied the Zoque versions, as well, and Mikeas answered my many questions about both. In her Spanish versions, she uses several Zoque names and terms, explaining them in footnotes. Rather than reproduce those footnotes in English, I have incorporated some of the definitions into my translations. Others I will note briefly here, in the order they appear in the poems. Piogbachuwe is the guardian of a volcano that is a central feature of Zoque territory. Kopajktzoka is a character in Zoque legend – a headless woman. Tzitzungätzüjk is the Chichonal Volcano and is female. Jakima'käjtzäjk is the Jakima Mountain, and is male. Nasakobajk is Mother Earth. Tzuan' is the parallel world where human souls go after death, but it can also be visited during life, 'at the invitation of the guardians of peaks and mountains', Mikeas explains.

## *From* Mokaya
## *One*

I am woman
and I celebrate every crease of my body
every tiny atom that makes me
where my hopes and doubts sail
All my contradictions are marvellous
because they are mine
I am woman and I celebrate every vein
where I trap my ancestors' secrets
all the Zoque men's words in my mouth
all the Zoque women's wisdom in my spit

## Two

I name myself and speak for all the mistreated girls
who gamble their innocence
in a darkened alley
For them May's first rain
and the wolf's roar
For them the tigress's howl
and the honeysuckle scent of tenderness
May mother quail and father sparrowhawk
soothe the souls of all the wounded girls
since the beginning of masculine time
May Piogbachuwe and Kopajktzoka come
to show us the beauty of the great beyond


## Three

I name myself and speak for all the raped girls
who seek their childhood in a bumblebee's buzz
and in a palm tree's sway
I speak in the name of the female volcano
Tzitzungätzüjk
and the male mountain
Jakima'käjtzäjk

I speak of the soul
its immortality untouchable by shame or doubt
I speak of immaculate sex
of the perennial girls

who soar above their grief
like the condor and eagle
showing their magnificence
dimmed with the passage of time


## Four

I speak of my mother
whose nagual crouches under Piogbachuwe's skirt
while her childhood is a howler monkey
leaping among stands of bamboo
I think of my mother
yes, I think of her
and her chestnut scent from the kitchen
in her nearly blind, inviolable
tenderness
I think of my mother
and she thinks of her alcoholic father
who waits for the northern wind as a sign of rain
who waits to see my grandmother naked at the river once again
at the age of sixteen

# MARTÍN RANGEL

Translated by Lawrence Schimel

Martín and I met in the Canadian Rockies, when we both took part in the Banff International Literary Translation Centre residency in 2017. I was working on my translation into English of the Equatorial Guinean writer Trifonia Melibea Obono's novel *La Bastarda*. Martín was the Mexican student fellow (the programme invites one student each from Canada, the US, and Mexico each year) who was translating into Spanish the alt-lit American poet Mira Gonzalez. Martín, in his early 20s, had already published four poetry collections, and also released sound performances under the name R V N G E L, although this was the first book-length translation project he was undertaking.

One night a week, members of our group gathered with snacks and drinks and listened as we gave readings from our own writing. Often someone from the group would translate the work into English, Spanish and French (which were the working languages at BANFF) so they'd be read in both the original and at least one translation. It was at one of these nights that I first heard Martín (who usually comes across as quite timid) and his electrifying performances, and when I first started translating some of his work into English.

While I started translating his poetry, the first of my translations of his work to be published was prose. When Sabotage Reviews announced the anthology *Verbs that Move Mountains: Essays and Interviews on Spoken Word Cultures Around the World*, edited by Claire Trévien, I told Martín about the project and he wrote about the Mexican spoken-word scene.

These poems come from a collection forthcoming from Broken Sleep on the last day of this year, and are the first poems from it to be published.

## 'Time Passes Slower When You Can't Sleep' Science Confirms

and we never finish watching the sun go down
and we were never all dying it was a performance
we close our eyes and could see flowers but not smell them
i remember an interminable face of sweat and flitter
and music playing strongly          to be just
body   i remember i crossed through the mirror and there was
nothing
on the other side of things   don't miss many
common things like insomnia or eclipses
or fractures of the chest or not encouraging medical diagnoses
or the fear of insomnia
                              (which sometimes is worse)
of all the things i've forgotten over time
*how to live*   is the one i most miss
but i am sure that someone has already posted
a tutorial on youtube about this
which will hardly show me how to live
but will sure amuse my insomnia

## Big Data

everything passes and
we are all passengers
      of the same
suicidal vehicle

never trust your instincts

      please take
your elbows off the table

lift your chin

      and smile

don't forget that you're being recorded

# SARA URIBE

Translated by JD Pluecker

*Antígona González* is the story of the search for a body, a specific body, one of the thousands of bodies lost in the war against drug trafficking that began more than a decade ago in Mexico. A woman, Antígona González, attempts to narrate the disappearance of Tadeo, her elder brother. She searches for her brother among the dead. San Fernando, Tamaulipas, appears to be the end of her search. But Sara Uribe's book is also a palimpsest that rewrites and cowrites the juxtapositions and interweavings of all the other Antigones. From the foundational *Antigone* of Sophocles passing through Griselda Gambaro's *Antígona furiosa*, Leopoldo Marechal's *Antígona Vélez*, María Zambrano's *La tumba de Antígona* all the way to *Antigone's Claim* by Judith Butler. And this book's writing machine includes testimonies from family members of the victims and fragments and fragments from news stories that provide accounts of all these absences, all the bodies that we are missing. *Antígona González* was translated by JD Pluecker and published in the United States by Les Figues Press in 2016.

# From *Antígona González*

*Here we are all invisible. We have no face.*
*We have no name. Here our present seems suspended.*
*I'll wake up at any moment, I say when I try to lie to myself, when I can't stand*
*it anymore, when I'm about to collapse.*
*But that moment never comes: what happens here is what is actually real.*
*They told me they'd found a few corpses, that there was a chance. They told me*
*that they were going to bring them here.*

What thing is the body when someone strips it of a name, a history, a
family name? *That there was a chance.* When there is no face or trail or
traces or signs. *That they were going to bring them here.* What thing is the
body when it's lost?

I came to San Fernando to search for you, Tadeo. I came to see if one of
these bodies was yours.

How is a body recognized? How to know which is the right one if it is
under ground and in piles? If the halflight. If the ashes. If this thick
mud steadily covers it all. How to claim you, Tadeo, if the bodies here
are just debris?
This pain is also mine. This fasting.
The absurd, the exhausting, the urgent labor of unburying a body to
bury it anew. To confirm out loud what is so feared, so desired: yes sir,
agent, yes sir, medical examiner, yes sir, police officer, this body is mine.

Some by their tattoos. Others their scars.
Some by the clothes they wore the last day they were seen, some by
their teeth and some recognizable only by their DNA.
The ones who faint prior to glimpsing the doorway, as if their eyes were
prevented from identifying their loved one in the formless matter.
There are some who search as a way to refuse to remain in the silence
to which they've been relegated.
There are some who inquire time and time again as a means to
confront their misfortune.

I'm also disappearing, Tadeo.
And all of us here, if your body, if the bodies of our people.
All of us here will gradually disappear if no one searches for us,
if no one names us.
All of us here will gradually disappear if we just look helplessly at each
other, watching how we disappear one by one.

# OSCAR DAVID LÓPEZ

Translated by Leo Boix

I came across the work of Óscar David López while researching
LGBTQI+ contemporary poets from Latin America. I was immedi-
ately struck by López's combative irreverence. His sensuous and
chameleonic poems are brimming with sharp irony, heightened by an
eccentric use of grammar. 'The poet has to be like a transvestite, to
put themselves in the high heels and clothes of the other in order to
be able to transmit that experience to the reader. Not only as an
exercise for the poet and their ego, but also for readers so they can
find themselves in that poetry', explained the poet in a recent
interview published in Mexico. López is a transvestite and suffers
from a long-term inflammatory condition that keeps him in hospital
for several months every year. Both of these realities become subjects
that he has explored in great detail with books such as *Farmacotopía*
(2014) and *Cancer Queen* (2019).

The poet born in Monterrey (Nueva León) has published nine
books of poetry, as well as a novel, essays, articles, and many collabo-
rations with visual artists. The two poems included here belong to his
first poetry collection, *Gangbang* (2007), a compelling debut reminis-
cent of the work of E.E. Cummings that explores notions of
pornography, homoerotic desire and illness. Lopez finds his voice
while whimsically nodding to some of his literary and visual inspira-
tions, from the Argentinean poet Nestor Perlongher, the Spanish
author Antonio Gamoneda, the US poet, novelist and playwright
William Carlos Williams to the artists Pieter Brueghel and Jean
Cocteau.

## Boy Masturbating In The Window

the currency is interchangeable
like a litre of blood

a book you lend
knowing that you will lose it

the stare that desires
node

some people stretch their veins
while
loving

and read something sad
like the sides of a coin

their breathing
fogs up the city

borrowed bodies
getting to know each other intimately

cold crystals
inhabited by limit

reminding me
before the absence

the colour red
like the title of a book

that only I
know


## On A Drawing By Jean Cocteau

yes to sailors and cooks on pillows
you will no longer find themselves stripping:
oh, jean cocteau
visit me in the early evening
and give me new lips
slow capers
form
– you give without wanting: giving in
real thirst
        like a cook called
just by the word knife
needing the edge:
unleash me from these drops

# ELENA PONIATOWSKA

Translated by Cynthia Steele

This text is from Elena Poniatowska's only book of poetry to date, *Rondas de la niña mala* (The Naughty Girl's Nursery Rhymes), published in 2008, which is made up of a series of intimate portraits of the author's relationship with her family in Mexico City during the 1940s. Mexico's most celebrated living author, Poniatowska was born in Paris in 1932 and moved to Mexico City at the age of ten to escape the Second World War. Descended from the Polish royalty and the Mexican aristocracy, she has devoted her life to advocating for women artists and activists and for the dispossessed, as well as for democratisation. Her books available in English translation include *Lilus Kikus and Other Stories* (1954), *Here's to You, Jesusa* (1969), *Massacre in Mexico* (1971) – famously about the repression of the 1968 student protests in Mexico City – *Tinísima* (1991), *Leonora* (2012), and *The Heart of the Artichoke* (2012). Poniatowska's most recent novel, *El amante polaco* (2019), juxtaposes the history of her Polish ancestors with her own autobiography. She has received every major literary prize in the Spanish-speaking world, including the Premio Cervantes in 2013.

## Open Heaven

Last night God climbed
into my mother's bed,
he lifted up the sheet
and tossed her outside.

God tends to do such things
to His chosen ones.
He hungers
for mystical raptures,
scanning the crowd for blank faces.
My mother's face compensates him for
psychoanalysis, psychedelics,
long marches down the tunnel of time,
rockets invading the stratosphere,
Cape Canaveral and Disneyland.

God is convinced
that the world
was born with him.

The fierceness of his desire
overshadows my mother.
He lets go of the straps,
sending her back to childhood.
He calls her on the phone,
making her punch the clock.

God is persuaded that
we're all conspiring against him.

My mother is a lunatic.
God takes her by the shoulders,
shakes her, ruffles her hair,
disturbs the hive.
Her eyes are deep wells
where God whets his conscience.
I wish I could die when
Santa Teresita del Niño Jesús
speaks from her mouth,
that little prune-faced saint
who would sip away the spit
of the consumptives.

God thinks he is
better than anyone.

Open mouths of women taking communion,
their tender tongues wet with saliva.
Christianity is a hot
breath, hospital vapors,
an endless antechamber
to see the minister.

Sanctity is some incomprehensible shit.

My mother leans over
to kiss me good night.
Her eyes burn a hole in my face,
my cheeks turn red with shame.
Momma, I just can't take so much God,
I want to shout,
tell Him you aren't a saint, that you belong to me,
he has so many brides.
Ask Him who made Him, where he's from,
what plots He hatched up in Heaven.
Momma, who made God? How lovely is reason.
Tell Him I'm the one who sees you
performing your ablutions, how you send me away
with the roses
so they won't die in the night.


If it were up to me, God, I would demand
that you look for other mothers
to stamp with your seal
of foolishness.

# ELENA PONIATOWSKA

Translated by Amanda Hopkinson & Nick Caistor

Short interview with Elena Poniatowska about *Nursery Rhymes for a Naughty Girl*

**AMANDA HOPKINSON:** how come this is your only poetry collection? Did you write it in a rush, or did it take years?

**ELENA PONIATOWSKA:** When I was young, whenever I fell in love I wrote poems. I never gave them to my boyfriends, as I never thought them good enough. It was Octavio Paz who told me to get them published and who even helped to edit them.

**AH:** So you never wrote poems again, or did you write more, without thinking of publication?

**EP:** I don't think I've got any more poems, though you might come across one here or there in the pages of a book. I committed myself full-time to journalism, since that is what I lived from. I continued writing other books, and poetry took second place, even though I had an immense liking and admiration for Rosario Castellanos, Octavio Paz, Gabriel Zaid, and traditional poets such as Ramón López Velarde.

**AH:** How did you decide on a theme for this collection, or did it just come to you?

**EP:** When I collected all my poems together, I decided to call them *Nursery Rhymes of a Naughty Girl* so that no-one would expect formal verse or high poetry. It's a title based on childhood games which we played in a circle, or at hopscotch which in Mexico we call 'aeroplane', and other games we used to play and my grandchildren have played too.

**AH:** Did you grow up hearing 'nursery rhymes' and 'lullabies' at home?

**EP:** For the first ten years of my life, I only spoke French, my native language. There was one writer of children's books, the French Comtesse de Ségur, and I'm sure many children of my age read her books, they were also beautiful objects in themselves.

**AH:** Is there anything in particular you might like to add concerning 'Guardian Angel'?

**EP:** I'd kept it to myself until one day Octavio Paz came round for a meal at my parents' house. He asked me to show him what I was writing, adding: 'Of course you've got some poems'. So I showed them him and he liked them and ERA, the publishing house which had published my first books, *Hasta no verte Jesús mío* and *La Noche de Tlatelolco* decided to bring them out.

# Guardian Angel

My mother advises me
to leave the window
wide open
to allow him in,
the Guardian Angel.

Behind my bedhead
the Angel
breathes
with his wings.

In France,
the Angel
– of white porcelain –
would smile
with cherry-red lips.

Tissue paper
straw and paste
a touch of purple,
each one typifies
the Mexican Angel.
The avenging Angel
trumpeting rebellion.
In a single wingbeat
his hair bristles on end,
his head is crowned
with a newspaper ship.

He distributes to the four winds
blood-red cuttings.

Newsboy Angel
passers-by pierce him
with furious needles
beneath his feathers.

'You forgot your wings,'
says God on his return.
'How could I forget them
when they hurt me so?'

God reproves him.

In the night
he scatters starry headlines,
and into the bedroom brings
the Great Bear.

At dawn,
the Angel,
a pink flamingo,
turns pale.

He escapes
through the window
and leaves the heavens
devoid of constellations.

# TEDI LÓPEZ MILLS

Translated by JS Tennant

I first met Tedi López Mills at a literary festival in Xalapa, Mexico, in October 2012. I see that, in an interview I conducted with her there, she named T. S. Eliot, Xavier Villaurrutia, Gilberto Owen, Jorge Cuesta, Apollinaire and William Carlos Williams as writers she frequently returns to. Later, I worked with her on some translations for a bilingual anthology I co-edited for PEN International, *Write Against Impunity* (commissioned to commemorate murdered journalists across Latin America) and published, in *The White Review*, an excerpt from her remarkable, award-winning, collection *Death on Rua Augusta*, translated by David Shook.

López Mills was born in Mexico to a mother from the USA and studied in philosophy there and in France. She grew up bilingual and has translated work by Anne Carson, along with various others. These poems will feature in a forthcoming book provisionally called *Against Harmony*, one whose title gives something of their disjunctive nature, characteristic of her work in general. Drawing, perhaps, on her dual heritage and close affinities for Anglophone traditions, the collection will contain cycles of poems in conversation (often with an ironic slant) with writers such as Ted Hughes, Adrienne Rich and Ezra Pound. It wasn't a surprise for me to find, following our conversations in 2012, the strong presence in in these recent poems of the Octavio Paz of El mono gramático and the Chilean master Raúl Zurita, two writers she cited then as abiding influences.

# A Harmonic Poem, Reflective, Descriptive

A harmonic poem, reflective, descriptive.
A place where monkeys screech in the trees
and dust clouds appear, whirlwinds, gullies,

*The view is yours if you want it*, it says.

A poem on the poem.
The white of the poem.
The black edge to the poem's surface.

You put thought in its place: it gets bored.
You write the chronicle of fixity:
'learning to keep still'.

The critique of rhetoric
is read diagonally
so as not to highlight
the rhetoric.

For example: that the eyes
of the spirit see the poem
and not the eyes of the flesh
which are those one
sees in the mirror
with one's own eyes.

The plot is confusing.

Movement is no metaphor for change.

The poet goes among the stones with his whip.
He shouts at the monkeys to scare them.
The monkeys hide in the undergrowth and watch him.
The poet seeks meanings.

Nothing is no metaphor for emptiness.

In the figurative backdrop of the palace
there is incredulity at the minutiae
of descriptions and the bizarre
absence of outcomes.

The poet comes to a hole in the road.

A moment is no metaphor for time.

*On the inside of the palace*, he says to me scornfully.

To regard the thrush
sidelong
through the corner of
the flesh eyes
is nearly the same
as possessing it
with the spirit.

The poet does not believe in reality
if it is not represented
within the dialectic he proposes.

One thing is no metaphor for another.

The poet struggles
in the landscape of imperfection:
'the tendrils of letters'.
Words do not eat words.

## The Sensation of Recalling Something Forgotten is One...

The sensation of recalling something forgotten is one
of the effects that good poetry should give us.
I read slowly and later recite the poem with eyes closed
so that the memory in the image of this half afternoon
should call up comes clean and quickly.
Remembering things forgotten. The shack on the border. That of the
mother.
That of the father. That of vertigo on the bridge.
My head vacant, episodic. That of the father drowned with his daughter.
That of the mother watching from the bank as they sink in the river.
*Flashes of light* – writes Zurita – *almond-coloured meat.*
Forty-five degrees in the shade of a dead tree.
I'm going to place myself in the midst of this poem's story.
It's not a memory but the stillness of an incident in a photograph
at six in the morning. I recite the memory. The father wades out. The black
shirt snags on a post. A piece of rubber floats among the foam with its
yellowed fringes like singed paper on a grey surface. *I weep for an enemy land.*
To be clear: what I think is not the same as what I feel.

# ENRIQUETA OCHOA

Translated by Anthony Seidman

The poet Enriqueta Ochoa (1928–2008) was born in Mexico's northern region, in the city of Torreon. Belonging to the same generation as Rosario Castellanos and Jaime Sabines, Ochoa produced a poetry that shares some similarities with her more famous peers – especially for passages that veer on the 'confessional' – yet her verse is decidedly more oneiric and numinous, and less conversational. She counted Saint John of the Cross and Saint Teresa of Avila as the wellsprings for her own poetry. For decades, she published little, preferring to hone her craft, all while loathing self-promotion and publicity. Ochoa considered her poetry to be: 'the discovery of the unusual in the everyday. After having descended to the deepest areas of being, beyond the crossing of the subconscious, where the sublime and the terror go hand in hand, the word names the essence and existence of man. It is the world of experiences that best configures symbols, magic, images, the liberation of concrete words'. Indeed, contemporary poets like Elsa Cross have pointed out Ochoa as one of the few true ecstatic voices in 20th century Mexican poetry.

She is now widely celebrated in Mexico. Her reputation continues to grow, especially among younger poets. The poems in this selection come from *Retorno de Electra* (1978), which can be considered as her 'selected poems'.

## Power, War

*For Efrain Huerta and Thelma Nava*

You are the gold record, bestselling,
spinning on the phonograph
from the darkness of time.
The serrated knife removing scales

from the gold fish;
the eyelashes of wisdom
from the earth's hide;
eyes of blue fire
from the balloon of hope.

You send them equipped, with a slogan,
to Death.
And there She goes, blind,
with all of her prostitution supine,
eyes curdled,
on her great gala night.

Everybody starts from the roots,
reverberates, shaking the neighboring roots.
Man is always this neighboring root
that shudders helplessly, convulsed;
holding in his breath,
because he feels that on top of his stem,
above the flower that sings,
in the very pool of fronds
where light dozes its green tremor,
the pages of history are being dictated.
There is an untouchable flock
sitting on the dark nest of death,
a nest packed with eggs
ovulating man.

# JUANA KAREN PEÑATE

Translated by Wendy Call and Sarah Van Arsdale

Juana Karen Peñate writes poems in the Tumbalá variant of Ch'ol, a Mayan language spoken in Chiapas, and self-translates them into Spanish. The poem 'Opposing Silence' is from her 2002 collection, *Mi nombre ya no es silencio* (Silence is No Longer My Name). 'I Belong to the Night' and 'Chajk' are from *Ipusik'al matye'lum / Corazón de selva* (Forest Heart) published in 2013.

Chajk is the name of Ch'ol diety who manifests as lightning – the power of the lightning bolts demonstrating his mood. Sometimes he's young and rash, and other times older and more measured in his power.

Of 'I Belong to the Night', Peñate says, 'When I am caught up in my obligations as a daughter, as a mother, as a woman, I go out at night to walk'. This time with 'the universe of the night' brings her peace.

'Opposing Silence' was inspired by a time when Peñate was living away from her hometown and received alarming news of violent conflict between the Ch'ol and another indigenous community – exacerbated by relentless military and corporate activity in the region.

These are the first poems that we have co-translated. We passed drafts back and forth, working from the Spanish versions of the poems. We compiled a list of questions for Peñate and then enjoyed a long Zoom discussion with her, in which she explained some elements of the Ch'ol poems, as well as the poems' contexts. These are the first English translations of Peñate's poetry to be published.

## I Belong to the Night

Night envelops me,
as I tuck into my trembling words.
The night is awake,
watching me intently.
She has come for me.
My Ch'ol words fracture and fill my mouth.
New blood shadows and swells my veins.
Nothing is cold now I belong to the night.


## Chajk

Radiate your force down to me, Chajk
I'm the power in your lightning.
Wrest impossible words from me.
Decipher me.
Question me with wind's breath
as I cannot,
searching the endless sky
searching in my dreams
for my voice, quickening.

## Opposing Silence

Enough of the abuse of this village.
Who listens to a voice from the boundless jungle mountains?
I walk; with only my own echoes reverberating.

How far does my voice carry?
How to oppose the silence?
From the jungle to the city,
there's no way out, say the Ch'ols, the Tseltals,
the Tsotsils, the Tojolabals.

Could the poets' words reach those who rule the earth?
No, the poets raise their songs into air, into darkness,
into pouring rains, to life and to death.

How can we make the dishonorable understand?
The blood of our veins flows on the wind,
powerful as song.

We'll raise our voices as one,
the music of our jungles soothing hate,
our canyons' silence razing walls,
our languages unifying,
melting the greed that wants us dead

# JEANNETTE L CLARIOND

Translated by Samantha Schnee

In *The Goddesses of Water* Jeannette Clariond draws on the mythology of pre-Hispanic Mexico to lament the epidemic of femicides that began at the close of the twentieth century in that country and shows no sign of ceasing. Part One, 'Antecanto', introduces Coyolxauhqui, the moon goddess, sister of all goddesses of water, and closes with the image of a hummingbird. Because of its speed, the hummingbird was known as the messenger and guardian of time. It also symbolised love, happiness and beauty. With its abilities to drink from flowers and fly backwards, like those who are trying to reconcile with their past, it is omnipresent in Central American poetry.

Part Two, 'Who Were These Goddesses', is typeset as an inverse pyramid, a reflection of the Pyramid of the Moon referenced in the 'Antecanto'. It references a number of important cultural artefacts: Jade (which the goddesses carry beneath their tongues) was more valuable than gold, and symbolised eternity. The quetzal, a sacred bird, symbolized the god Quetzalcóatl, who represented the duality implicit in Mesoamerican cosmogony: the union of heaven and earth; spiritual and physical.

The poem employs a number of Nahuatl words. The description of the goddesses' breasts as buds of *omexóchitl* refers to the flower of dusk, that represented the spirit of Quetzalcótal; in Nahuatl *ome* means two and *xochitl* means flower. *Ámatl* is paper dating to pre-Columbian times in Central America, handmade from the bark of white and red jonote trees, boiled with lime. *Tona* is solar heat, a term frequently used in reference to female deities (encompassing fecundity and powerful sexuality), such as the goddess Coatlicue, also called Tonantzin, the mother of Earth.

The manuscript has five parts, the body of which is formed by fifty two tercets, called 'fragments', reflecting the fragmentation of the female body in both the pre-Hispanic Mexican myth and, tragically, in Mexican society today. According to the *New York Times,* femicides in Mexico increased ten percent between 2018 and 2019, and from seven per day in 2017 to ten per day in 2019.

## *Antecanto*

Ur-darkness. From its depths a fine radiance appears and splits the shadows in two. The light is not of heavenly origin, nor are the shadows divine: both emanate from the blue-hued, broken center of the ruins.

Coyolxauhqui, goddess of the moon, presages the birth of this light: thrown from the top of the temple by her brother the Sun, he decapitates her, throwing her head into the sky as her body falls in pieces to Earth. This fall prefigures her destiny: illuminating and creating order in the Cosmos. The goddess embarks on her journey toward the light: a tale of water and fire, dreams and life.

During the twenty-eight days of her transit, throughout various phases, she illuminates the dark firmament but remains invisible for three. Is she dead? Silence and fear rule the Earth; if the Moon does not appear, all will become inscrutable, nocturnal writing.

The fall of this goddess, sacrificial mystic, reclaims death of the body, a body that must die to be reborn into the light. Her dismemberment symbolizes the successive phases of the Moon in endless darkness. When she becomes invisible, water trembles increasingly on Earth. The Moon fertilizes and is fertile. Woman and mirror, she gathers that which dispels horror.

Coyolxauhqui's fate is best appreciated when Venus reaches her zenith: when she casts her play of light and shadow on the

Pyramid of the Moon, she affirms that we are both black and white, united in a nexus of internal movement, nucleus that harvests the ruins, the diaspora, the chaos that follows the fall. Her mysticism so intense that her light is a step, a footprint, the celebration of a destiny.

And like Venus, we are light and shadow, a dialectic of free will that endows the myth with fundamental meaning. Diurnal or nocturnal, the star will surely change signs: the tension between twilights is established at dawn or at dusk, poetic spirit-material in steady equilibrium. To accept this tension is to live in the unforgiving chiaroscuro of creation, communion between heavenly beings and those of the underworld who penetrate and procreate on Earth, reconciling the inaugural relations of the universe, always at risk of resurrection in a new cosmic oneness – mystery of the duality that overcomes knowledge which has yet to recognize our soul.

Each month Coyolxauhqui gives life – water – and leaves, to return again. She is all light, then she is extinguished bit by bit. What is the meaning of this fragmentation? What is the beauty inherent in this myth? We have known neither how to read her light, nor how to move forward in darkness.


The goddesses of water accompany us on a journey through rivers, rites, mountains, rain, shaping our faces and restoring our innocence in the clear waters of creation. They wash the song. Their voices, florescence in slow rain, enter a timeless past intending to unite dawn with night. Their Home is in the damp sky. Soft chalice, touching our lips to tell of modest water. They sing the soft breeze, churning rivers for their lips of quartz.

Listen to them: the fluttering of a hummingbird at the first light of dawn.

# Who Were These Goddesses

They were so called because they wore god's mask, and because their faces and hearts were
resolute as stone. For days, years, they walked with jade beneath their tongues, seeking
Home. They worked the land and bejeweled their bodies. Not as a sign of vanity, but
because they tended the amaranth in their yearning for fire. Xiuhtecuhtli was their
god; xiuhtlatoa their language, meaning 'words of fire' – that which ignites the
heart. They were careful not to use xaltlatoa, 'words of sand', fleeting, vague
and un-understandable. At night they accompanied the Sun on his descent.
They were jade, translucency, they purified the underworld, deciphering
destiny. Their essence dwelt in the Afterlife. Their petals arose in song.
They adorned their Home with hymns and flowers and filled their
desire with vision, fine chalice of the sagacious seed. The upper
half of their bodies naked; their breasts were buds of omexóchitl
and their verdant dreams the sprigs of a birch. From their legs
blossomed the pure white feathers of the quetzal. Coatlicue,
the goddess mother, gave birth to the Sun and the Moon.
With a sword of fire, the Sun beheaded the Moon and
tossed her body down the steps, shattering it in a
thousand pieces, Coyolxauhqui covered head to
toe in shining rattles of vipers. She fell and
entered darkness. And so it was recorded
on the tree of ámatl: Light and shadow
will not last. So says the history of
woman: she sought to recreate
what was within her to
rewrite the Book:

The song will be reborn in each body in such a way that we learn to redefine what is ours,
as our daughters will, too, and our daughters' daughters, and their daughters'
daughters will know that their bodies are light on Earth, heat of the sun
with its tona, energy, fecundity, song that dances along the perimeter
of stars. And so, they watch over us from the firmament at dusk
and dawn as the sun is born and dies. These goddesses of
water were destined to be masters of their own desire,
guides of their own light. We must engrave on our
hearts: *The place where goddesses are born.*

## *We are the Land*

Karen McCarthy Woolf reviews *When the Light of the World Was Subdued, Our Songs Came Through: A Norton Anthology of Native Nations Poetry,* edited by Joy Harjo with Leanne Howe, Jennifer Elise Foerster and contributing editors, W. W. Norton & Company, 2020.

> 'WE BEGIN WITH THE LAND. We emerge from the earth of our mother, and our bodies will be returned to earth. We are the land. We cannot own it, no matter any proclamations by paper state. We are literally the land, a planet. Our spirits inhabit this place. We are not the only ones. We are creators of this place with each other.' Joy Harjo (Introduction)

Throughout 2019–20 I was a Fulbright scholar in residence at the Promise Institute for Human Rights at UCLA, exploring how law and poetry might combine to express safe spaces in complex environments. Any public event we held or attended started with an acknowledgement of the University of California's status as a land-grant institution. This means it sits on land, 'given' by the state, that is the ancestral home of the indigenous Gabrielino-Tongva peoples. Although I have always considered the US to be a colonial settler-nation, it was the first time I had physically experienced a formal recognition of that occupation. These were solemn, ceremonial moments, which in their utterance acknowledge and embody culture and continuance in the face of genocide.

It is in this spirit that this anthology, the first of its kind to be published by Norton (whose compilations have long denoted the canon), opens with a blessing 'Prayer for Words' from N Scott Momaday. This precedes an introduction by its chief editor Joy Harjo, whose second tenure as the first indigenous Poet Laureate of the US has illuminated a literature, without knowledge of which, to re-attribute Toni Morrison, the body of American writing is rendered 'bereft'.

The book's architecture mirrors its intent as a work of decolonisation, where the established borders between art forms are necessarily blurred to incorporate poets whose practice also embraces music, installation, visual art, sculpture, political, legislative and environmental activism. Spoken word and its performative poetics are privileged as opposed to ghettoised, laying flat the artificial hierarchies that seek to divide and rule meta-literary cultures whose histories, customs and religion are held in living archives of orality and song.

As Harjo explains: '...we have organized this collection into five geographical regions. We employed the Muscogean directional path, which begins East to North and continues to the West and then to the South.' Cumulatively, this takes the reader through 573 tribal nations and 161 poets, spanning four centuries, who together speak more than 150 indigenous languages, some of which are presented in translation. There are also introductory essays and historical texts at the beginning of each section.

The rotation commences in the 'Northeast and Midwest' from Maine to Iowa via Peter Blue Cloud's (Mohawk) shamanic 'Rattle' and Linda Legarde Grover's (Anishinaabe) elegy to languages lost in 'Everything You Need to Know in Life You'll Learn in Boarding School'.

Next, in 'Plains and Mountains', we alight on poems of political lyric that 'sing, narrate, and argue' (Heid E Erdrich). Layli Longsoldier's (Oglala Lakota) '38' bears witness to the mass execution of the Dakota 38, who were hanged on Boxing Day at the orders of Abraham Lincoln in the same week he signed The Emancipation Proclamation. It, like Lois Red Elk's (Isanti, Hunkpapa, Ihanktonwa)

'Our Blood Remembers', holds its focus amid atrocity, to recount a grief in the people and the earth where 'a quiet wind covered the | lands weeping softly like an elderly woman, shawl | over bowed head.' To the non-indigenous reader, this quotation might appear metaphorical or anthropomorphic: from a native nations perspective that weeping is literal.

Global ecological concerns, that are intensifying as capitalist America flounders in the glare of its own denial, are also centred, to demonstrate a cooperative friendship with land and other animals that transcends the inherent contradictions of the pastoral. In 'Pacific Northwest, Alaska and Pacific Islands' for example, the sea and waterways are significant characters. Here we find 'Prayer Song Asking for a Whale' told in St Lawrence Island Yup'ik, together with poet and language scholar Nora Marks Dauenhauer's (Tlingit) 'How to Make Good Baked Salmon from the River' which she notes is 'best made in dry fish camp on a beach' but is adapted 'for the city baked in an electric oven'.

This reach towards urban life and its emblematic modernity is an important strand, given that acts of historical retention are pressurised by a romanticisation that risks both stereotype and contemporary erasure. The editors counter these vulnerabilities by restricting the circle of inclusion to poets with official tribal membership, a decision that seeks to redress issues of appropriation and identity fraud. Natalie Diaz (Mojave/Gila River) satirises such societal tropes in 'When My Brother Was an Aztec', a poem in long, staggered tercets that juxtaposes the mythologies of the ancient 'Southwest and West' with a lived reality to dazzling ironic effect.

At times I wanted to check the publication dates (listed in 'Credits') to quickly locate the work against other literary movements and eras and wished they'd been printed below each poem, but this chronological intervention may well have interrupted a paradigm that places elders at the beginning of each geographic section and proceeds accordingly, concluding in the 'Southeast'.

This section follows a trajectory from 19th-century formal verse (Peter Perkins Pitchlynn (Choctaw), Joshua Ross and Lily Lee (Cherokee) through to Louis Little Coon Oliver's (Mvskoke) concrete poem 'The Sharp Breasted Snake' via Linda Hogan (Chickasaw) and contributing editor Leanne Howe (Choctaw), whose 'Noble Savage Sees a Therapist' is the ideal precursor to Joy Harjo's (Mvskoke) 'Rabbit is up to Tricks' where the protagonist creates an insatiably destructive clay man 'with no ears.' It is a fable that echoes the anthology's provocation to listen, with attention, to the songs of its contributors. At $19.95 it's affordable enough for every library, school and university to have no excuse but to stock it.

# Forms of Resistance

Stephanie Sy-Quia reviews *How the First Sparks Became Visible*
by Simone Atangana Bekono, translated by David Colmer,
The Emma Press, 2021
*Embrace* by Najwan Darwash, translated by Atef Alshaer
and Paul Batchelor, Poetry Translation Centre, 2020.
*Deviant Disciples: Indonesian Women Poets*, edited by Intan
Paramaditha, Tilted Axis, 2020.

The introduction to *Deviant Disciples* has a different title from its
cover or first page. It reads 'Deviant Disciples: Feminist Resistance in
Indonesian Poetry'. The impetus behind this short selection is the
Balinese tale of Calon Arang, a witch who lived in the 11th century.
Enraged when no one will marry her daughter, she looses deadly
disease upon the community. And she had seven students – or
disciples. Her presence both counters the recent trend of upholding
European witches as feminist foremothers (through bringing
attention to other, non-white witchcraft traditions), and universalises
it: everywhere, women can be seen organising in ways unsanctioned
by male faith or society leaders, dealing in epistemologies
beyond male control. The shift in emphasis, also, on this secondary
title, from 'Feminisms' to 'Feminist Resistance' situates the book in
a defiant mode. Not too much should be made of this, however, as
the chapbook is part of a series of others under the same auspices
of 'translating feminisms': others include samplings from Korean,
Vietnamese, Nepali, Tamil and the writings of various Filipina poets.
The Tilted Axis website offers the following on the project, which
has been funded through Arts Council England and Kickstarter:

*Translating Feminisms* showcases intimate collaborations between some of Asia's most exciting women and nonbinary writers and translators: contemporary poetry of bodies, labour and language, alongside essays exploring questions such as, 'Does feminism translate?'.

As part of Tilted Axis's wider project of decolonisation through and of translation, and in response to seeing WoC authors' work misread through a white feminist lens, we want to re-imagine the possibilities of a fully intersectional, international feminism, and ensure authors have the creative agency to contextualise their own work.

The poets and translators chosen to represent Indonesian feminisms here are Toeti Heraty and Dorothea Rosa Herliany, tr. Tiffany Tsao, Zubaidah Djohar tr. Norman Erikson Pasaribu, Shinta Febriany and Hanna Francisca tr. Eliza Vitri Handayani. Some of them published their first works almost fifty years ago, others, such as Djohar, are younger. The sampling is, by its very nature, a slim one, and one wishes that Tilted Axis could be given more space to expand on such a worthy project, but editor Intan Paramaditha's introduction details a sensitive selection process, attuned to the dominance of Jakarta, the complications of Balinese identity, and the violent euphemisms of Formal Indonesian under the New Order. The imagery of the anthology sloshes from Heraty's poem, where Calon Arang is seen 'among the graves, garlanded in guts', to the proclamation in one of Herliany's poems of a desire to 'consummate my pleasure. | before I consummate you too, stabbing | your heart, ripping your dick apart'. This is an incantatory poetics of choked necks, crushed bones, blood, guts, gore, where women are victims and victors in turn, wishing retributional violence upon men.

The Palestinian poet Najwan Darwash's poems, presented here in facing-page translations by Atef Ashaer and Paul Batchelor, are tiny, with the bleached, long-tumbled feeling of the fragment. As such, they command a solemnity from the reader which might be that employed when approaching an inscription; a sparse, ancient text which has withstood the forces of time to deliver a simple message, or a haunting phrase in a timeless prosody. Here is 'Variation on a line by al-Ma'arri' in its entirety:

> My body is a blue the sky has long forgotten;
> my body is a garden lost to the spring.
> You, 'tailor of the universe',
> what would be lost by not sewing me?

The imagery recalls Pablo Neruda: simple, gorgeous, never fey or cheaply sentimental. The plight of Palestine is a through line of the work, from 'At a Poetry Festival' where other attendees's countries are listed beneath their names: 'Next to my name, nothing but 'Jerusalem'. || How frightening your name must be, my little country –'; to 'The Thieves': 'who would believe me when I say that that my country | with its mountains and sea | when I say they have been stolen?' These poems' sparsity makes these questions hang in the air all the more. At almost the exact midpoint of the collection is 'The Face of a Friend', dedicated to the late John Berger, which asks 'What is the history of art if not the face of a friend?' It is a rousing call for international solidarity enacted through the arts.

*How the First Sparks Became Visible* is the debut work of Dutch poet Simone Atangana Bekono, whose subsequent novel, *Confrontatie* (Confrontations) was published in September 2020. *When the First Sparks Became Visible* won the Poëziedebuutprijs Aan Zee for best first collection in 2018, and consists of nine numbered, titleless poems which reckon rangily with a racialising gaze. Bekono's speaker dodges the taxonomical implications of inhabiting a black body, declaring instead 'I am a single moustache hair', 'I am the white Western male's thought experiment', 'black people make their bodies smaller with big hair and tiny phones | and that is exhausting'. '[U]nbodied we walk from the dune to the dirt track', she writes, seeking rest from this exhaustion, and this is the impetus of the collection: the black body's need for rest and leisure, freedom not from itself but from what others might make it to mean. 'There was going to be a quest, or at least a certain scenario', the speaker tells us, weary of the ways black bodies are meant to excavate their pain for an overwhelmingly white editorial class which call the shots. But even in this weariness, there is a soft-spoken grace, a tempo of soft loops, a call for more capacious empathy: 'all bodies are symptoms of thought', explaining oneself takes 'diamonds of time and energy', but it can't be sacked off in favour of playing on the beach, because 'all black people identify with drowned people', beaches are not always spaces of leisure for them. This collection speaks with steely grace on its own terms, and looks forward to the expansion of space it shall enact for others.

# The First Step of Day

Charlie Louth reviews *Patches of Sunlight, or of Shadow: Safeguarded Notes 1952–2005* by Philippe Jaccottet, translated by John Taylor, Seagull Books, 2020.

The first two entries in Philippe Jaccottet's *Patches of Sunlight, or of Shadow*, only one for each of 1952 and 1953, both touch on the idea of making a new start, of 'trying again' or 'gathering one's thoughts'. This return to a beginning, the shedding of experience as a way of venturing out, is a figure underlying all his writing. His work is not like Eliot's, but like Eliot he seems to dream of 'a poetry so transparent that we should not see the poetry, but that which we are meant to see through the poetry'. The dream leads to a distrust of images and to a contradictory cultivation and cherishing of the simple, both in lifestyle and in written style. Jaccottet's writing is always ethical, in that getting one's life right and getting one's line right are essentially the same thing, or versions of one another.

In his reading, which we learn a lot about from his notebooks, he is constantly attentive to moments when everyday language modulates into poetry, that is into words which register and reveal the world for what it is, full of presence and promise. In another early note he observes that 'the essential and very mysterious thing is that there is a way of saying "mountain", for example, which reveals (behind it, in it?) something like Being, and another way of saying the word that cannot do this'. He even expresses this as a kind of equation: 'Being seems to be perceptible where there is the least amount of "poetry" in the formal sense of the term; that is, rhetorical figures, metaphors, ornaments.' Given this, the notebooks, selections from which have appeared at intervals since 1984 under the general title *La Semaison* (translated by Tess Lewis as 'Seedtime'), are a paradoxical resource: they are the place where the everyday might take the form of poetry, and they are the place where the kind of knowledge is accumulated that will have to be put off if the writing of a poem is to be possible.

*Patches of Sunlight* is a kind of *salon des refusés*, made up of 'safeguarded' notes passed over for the original *Semaison* volumes and of a few from later. But for that reason it's the only gathering to give virtually the whole span of Jaccottet's writing life, reaching from before he married and moved to the Drôme in south-eastern France in 1953 and late into his established reputation as one of the most celebrated and widely read of contemporary French poets. The French original of this volume came out in 2013, the year before his work was consecrated by appearing in the Pléiade series, a mark of distinction awarded to very few living writers. He died in February at the age of 95, the last of a generation that included Yves Bonnefoy, André du Bouchet, Louis-René des Forêts.

Jaccottet's work, whatever form it takes – as often short prose as verse, and including a significant body of criticism, also translation – is always a finely attentive interrogation of the world, a hesitant and patient attempt to eludicate and formulate in words moments where what he thinks of as the mystery of existence suddenly becomes palpable. He is a very visual poet: one of his best books is a meditation on the work of the Italian painter Giorgio Morandi (*The Pilgrim's Bowl*, also translated by John Taylor), but in most cases the encounters of his texts take place while out walking: it might be a fruit-tree in blossom or a particular quality of light or the warmth rising from the ground on a familiar path. The texts seek to understand what connects us to the world and to find a way of speaking about it without fixing it, to bring us up against something incomprehensible but undeniably there, though only apprehensible from time to time, seemingly by chance, at points where the fabric of habit is broken through. Walking then is also a model for writing, setting out again, tracing a way, creating the conditions in which the world might waver, momentarily, into focus. Jaccottet often speaks of poetry as a respiration, as a kind of breathing, which when it has found the right rhythm equates to and perhaps reveals the respiration of the world, what he sometimes refers to as a 'hidden order'. As he writes in a note from 1958: 'The mystery is also that the words have sometimes been found and that, instead of concealing the world, they reveal it. Almost everything that human beings say, and what they do, conceals the world'.

If the notebooks seem to be the quarry from which the 'works' are extracted, they are also, and more and more as the various forms of Jaccottet's writing converge over time, themselves the place where the works come into being. The form of the note seems perfectly suited to Jaccottet's desire to record, but not to arrest, the movements of life as he senses them, something like an artist's way with a sketchbook. Some of the notations are in verse lines, but most are prose noticings, memories, dreams, passages taken from reading and comments on it. There is a lot more about people than in the other parts of the oeuvre. The style is exact, careful, courteous and with an elegance which is still close to a spoken voice.

I'm not sure that John Taylor's translation always manages to catch this. He sticks very close, but that sometimes means introducing an awkwardness, a formality, which seems to stray from the tone of Jaccottet's voice, which is one of gradual, intimate attunement to his subject. It's easy to imagine that it is a kind of devoutness on the part of the translator that has led to a slight estrangement of the English, producing a false note from time to time. A 'dream home' and 'l'habitation rêvée' are miles apart. Talking of Morandi, the English runs: 'They are things painted in the intimate room, in the 'room of the heart' – as this is not the

case of almost any other modern *oeuvre*'. What is the intimate
room? And why not say 'as is the case with almost no other modern
*oeuvre*'? It is the wish to trace out the French without making the little
adjustments needed to bring it more securely across. But the sentence
continues just as faithfully, and without faltering: 'as near the centre
as possible, whence the quiet radiance of the paintings and their frail
majesty'.

All this might seem rather remote. But in the most striking
moment of a documentary made for Swiss television in 1975 (available
on youtube) Jaccottet gives a wonderful defence of poetry's ability,
through its own disruptive coherence and 'accord', to create a
counter-image to what is wrong with the world and so resist it. And
if it cannot do that, he says, we might as well give up on it. The title
of this book, combining light and shade, evokes an idea of balance
that is fundamental to the measure Jaccottet aims for in his work and
to his understanding of poetry as working against the negative weight
of the times. We can take leave of him by quoting a very short poem
from *Airs* (1967):

> Le souci de la tourterelle
> c'est le premier pas du jour
>
> rompant ce que la nuit lie

[The turtle dove's enquiry | it is the first step of day || breaking what
night had joined]

# NOTES ON CONTRIBUTORS

**JUANA ADCOCK** is a Mexican-born, Scotland-based, bilingual poet and translator. Her first book, *Manca*, was named by Reforma as one of the best poetry books of 2014. Her English-language debut, *Split* (Blue Diode Press, 2019), was awarded the PBS Winter Choice.

**PITA AMOR** (Guadalupe Teresa Amor Schmidtlein) was a strikingly talented poet, and a less talented dancer and actress. She developed an intricate rhyming structure, writing on metaphysical and personal themes with passion and panache.

**ROMALYN ANTE** is a Filipino-British, Wolverhampton-based author. She is co-founding editor of *harana poetry* and a poetry editor at *Ambit* magazine. Her debut collection is *Antiemetic for Homesickness* (Chatto & Windus).

**SARAH VAN ARSDALE**'s sixth book, a chapbook of her poems titled *Taken*, is forthcoming from Finishing Line Press in 2021. She's the author of four books of fiction, and a book-length poem, *The Catamount*. She teaches creative writing in the Antioch University-LA Low-residency MFA Program.

**JEAN-CLAUDE AWONO** is a Cameroonian poet, literary critic, teacher and Director of the publishing house, Éditions Ifrikiya. He is also President of *La Ronde des Poètes du Cameroun* and *Le Festival Internationale de Poésie des Sept Collines de Yaoundé*. He has performed his work globally.

**LOREDANA BOGLIÙN** writes in both Italian and Istriot and her work has been widely anthologised. She has received numerous prizes and collections include *Poesie* (1988), *Masere – Muretti a secco* (1993), *La trasparenza* (1996), *La peicia* (1997) and *Soun la poiana* (2000).

**LEO BOIX** is a bilingual Latinx poet and translator born in Argentina and based in the UK. *Ballad of a Happy Immigrant* (Chatto & Windus, 2021) is his debut English collection.

**MALIKA BOOKER** won the Forward Poetry Prize for Best Single Poem (2020). She is published alongside poets Sharon Olds and Warsan Shire in The Penguin Modern Poet Series 3: *Your Family: Your Body* (2017) and is founder of Malika's Poetry Kitchen.

**JACQUES BREL** (1929–1978) was a Belgian cabaret singer, literary songwriter, actor and director and one of the masters of the modern French chanson. His songs have been covered by a great number of artists in various languages, from Frank Sinatra to Nina Simone, Edith Piaf to David Bowie.

**DAVID BROADBRIDGE**'s previous translation from Danish is a selection of medieval ballads *Treading the Dance* (Stacey 2011). His most recent collection of poems is *Something in Writing* (Oversteps Books 2017).

**WENDY CALL** is an author, editor, translator, and educator in Seattle (Duwamish land). Her poetry translations have been supported by the National Endowment for the Arts and the Fulbright Commission.

**NICK CAISTOR** is a British translator of over 80 books from Spanish, French and Portuguese. He is a three-time winner of the Premio Valle-Inclán for his translations. With his wife, Amanda Hopkinson, he has co-translated authors including Claribel Alegría (El Salvador), Paulo Coelho (Brazil) and Isabel Allende (Chile).

**INGER CHRISTENSEN** (1935–2009) is widely regarded as one of Denmark's foremost modernist poets through a career that included many collections – most notably *Det* (It) and *Sommerfugledalen* (Butterfly Valley).

**JEANNETTE CLARIOND** is a poet and translator who has dedicated much of her professional life to studying the thought and religion of ancient Mexico. A complete list of works is available on https://www.jeannettelclariond.com/libros-publicados-1

**GEORGINA COLLINS** is a freelance translator and consultant for the University of Bristol, and frequently works in Cameroon. She specialises in African literature and produced the first bilingual collection of Francophone African women's poetry, *The Other Half of History*.

**ADAM CZERNIAWSKI** born in 1934 in Warsaw, now lives in Wales. Publications include a memoir *Scenes from a Disturbed Childhood*, essays *Firing the Canon* and *Norwid's Selected Poems*. Recipient of the Norwid Foundation Medal and Poland's Gold Gloria Artis Medal.

**LIDIA DELTON** (née Belci) was born in Istria in 1951. She served as Dignano d'Istria's mayor 1993–2001. She has received numerous prizes from the Istria Nobilissima series, amongst others. Her collections are *Sulo parole cumo testamenti* (1998) and *Granai de pulvaro* (2005).

**WHITNEY DEVOS** has published translations of Martín Tonalmeyotl's poetry in *Latin American Literature today* and on the *World Literature Today* blog. Additional work is forthcoming in *Michigan Quarterly Review*.

**ADRIANA DÍAZ ENCISO** is a poet, author of fiction and translator.

**GUILLERMO FERNÁNDEZ** (1932–2012). Poet and translator. His translations of Italian literature earned him the Order of Merit of the Italian Republic. For decades, his workshops helped to form generations of new poets.

**LAURA FISK** is an NHS clinical psychologist, a poet and translator. Her latest publications are *Dancing Through a Pandemic* (New Feral Press, 2020), and *Coronavirus Chronicles* (PNV Publications, 2020) with translations into Macedonian by Juliana Velichkovska.

**WAYNE HOLLOWAY-SMITH** won The National Poetry Competition in 2018, and the Poetry Society's Geoffrey Dearmer Prize in 2017. His second collection, *Love Minus Love*, was published by Bloodaxe Books in 2020 and was shortlisted for the T.S. Eliot Prize.

**AMANDA HOPKINSON** is a writer, translator and academic. A former director of the British Centre for Literary Translation and professor of literary translation at the UEA, she has translated some 50 books, mainly by Latin American authors writing in Spanish and Portuguese.

**ELIN AP HYWEL** is a Welsh poet and translator, and a founding editor of Honno, the Welsh women's press. Her collected poems in Welsh, *Dal i Fod* (Still Here), edited by Menna Elfyn, was published by Barddas in 2020.

**ÓSCAR DAVID LÓPEZ** is a poet, novelist and essayist born in Monterrey, Nuevo León, in 1982. Among his poetry books are *Gangbang* (2007), *Roma* (2009), *Farmacotopía* (2014) and *Cancer Queen* (2019).

**CHARLIE LOUTH** teaches German at The Queen's College, Oxford. He has translated Hölderlin and Rilke and published recently *Rilke: The Life of the Work*.

**HARRY MAN** lives in North Yorkshire. His pamphlet 'Lift' won the UNESCO Bridges of Struga Award. *Deretter / Thereafter* with Endre Ruset is published by Flamme forlag in Norway and by Hercules Editions in the UK.

**TEDI LÓPEZ MILLS** was born in Mexico City, where she lives. Her books in English include *Death on Rua Augusta* (tr. David Shook), *Against the Current* (tr. Wendy Burk); a collection of essays is forthcoming. She has been awarded the Premio Xavier Villaurrutia and the Premio de Narrativa Antonin Artaud, among other prizes.

**CLAIRE MULLEN** is a writer, critic, and translator based in Mexico City. She is a current fellow with the National Book Critics Circle and an MFA candidate in nonfiction creative writing.

**ROBIN MYERS** is a Mexico City-based poet and translator of Latin American literature. She writes a monthly column on translation for *Palette Poetry.*

**ANDRÉ NAFFIS-SAHELY** is the author of *The Promised Land: Poems from Itinerant Life* (Penguin, 2017) and the pamphlet *The Other Side of Nowhere* (Rough Trade Books, 2019). He edited *The Heart of a Stranger: An Anthology of Exile Literature* (Pushkin Press, 2020) and is the editor of *Poetry London.*

**NILLANTHAN** lives and works in Yalpanam, Sri Lanka. He is an acclaimed poet, an artist who has exhibited widely on the sub-continent and a political analyst. Nillanthan was a witness to the final days of the civil war in Sri Lanka.

**CYPRIAN KAMIL NORWID** (1821–1883) was a Polish poet, dramatist, painter, and sculptor. He led a tragic, poverty-striken life and his talent was not recognised within his lifetime, but he is now considered one of the most important Polish Romantic poets.

**ENRIQUETA OCHOA** (1928–2008), was born in Mexico's northern region, in the city of Torreon. Her poetry is now widely celebrated in Mexico, with her reputation continuing to grow, especially among younger poets.

**NAHUI OLIN** (b. Carmen Mondragón, Mexico, 1893–1978) was a poet, painter, and artist's model active in Mexico City in the 1920s and '30s.

**JUANA KAREN PEÑATE** is a bilingual poet, educator, television producer, and activist from Tumbalá, Chiapas. Writing in Spanish and Ch'ol, she is author of four bilingual books of poetry, with two forthcoming in 2021.

**IRMA PINEDA**, author, translator, and professor from Juchitán, Oaxaca, has published seven books of bilingual Isthmus Zapotec-Spanish poetry. She is a member of the UN Permanent Forum on Indigenous Issues.

**JD PLUECKER** is a language worker who writes, translates, organizes, interprets, and creates. They have translated numerous books from the Spanish and their book of poetry and image, *Ford Over*, was released in 2016 from Noemi Press.

**ELENA PONIATOWSKA** is the most famous living author in Mexico, having published some 45 books of fiction and testimonial literature, most of which have also appeared in English translation. She has received every major literary prize in the Spanish-speaking world, including the Premio Cervantes in 2013.

**MARTÍN RANGEL** (Pachuca, 1994) is a Mexican poet, translator and internet artist. He has published seven books of poetry. Instagram: @martinrangel

**PAUL RODDIE** (Glasgow, 1971) studied modern languages at the University of Glasgow, before moving to France in 1995 where he teaches. He writes in and translates between French and English. His collections of bilingual poetry are *No Holds Bard / Terrains vagues, terrains précis* and *Taking the World by Storm / Le ravisseur du monde*. A collection of aphorisms in French is due in 2021.

**SOFÍA ROSALES** was born in Mexico City. She studied Graphic Design and Narrative Illustration at the UNAM, FAD. Her drawings can be found illustrating anthologies, articles, poems and digital content. She loves drawing mythology.

**ENDRE RUSET** is a poet, literary critic and translator from Molde, Norway. He has been awarded a Bjørnson Scholarship (2005) and the presitigious Bookkeeper Scholarship (2015). He was also shortlisted for the Bastian Award for Translation.

**MIKEAS SÁNCHEZ** (born Chiapas, 1980) is author of six bilingual (Zoque-Spanish) books of poetry and co-founder of ZODEVITE, which won Pax Christi's 2017 International Peace Prize for its anti-fracking activism.

**LAWRENCE SCHIMEL**'s most recent translation into English is María José Ferrada's *Niños: Poems for the Lost Children of Chile* (Eerdmans) and into Spanish is Maggie Nelson's *Bluets* (Tres Puntos).

**SAMANTHA SCHNEE**'s translation of *The Goddesses of Water* will be published by Shearsman in the UK in August and by World Poetry Books in the US in December. This year she joins the jury for the Stephen Spender Prize for poetry in translation.

**ANTHONY SEIDMAN** is a poet and translator from Los Angeles. Some full-length translations include *Smooth-Talking Dog: Poems of Roberto Castillo Udiarte*; *Caribbean Ants: Poems by Homero Pumarol*; *A Stab in the Dark* by Facundo Bernal, and *Confetti-Ash: Selected Poems of Salvador Novo*, co-translated with David Shook. He currently edits the Museum Poetica section for *Caesura*.

**CYNTHIA STEELE** is Professor Emerita of Comparative Literature at the University of Washington, Seattle. Translations include Inés Arredondo, *Underground Rivers and Other Stories* (Nebraska, 1996) and José Emilio Pacheco, *City of Memory and Other Poems* (City Lights, 2001, with David Lauer).

**CLARE SULLIVAN**, professor of Spanish at the University of Louisville, teaches poetry and translation. Her collaborative translations of Natalia Toledo and Enriqueta Lunez have appeared in Phoneme Media and Ugly Duckling Presse.

**GEETHA SUKUMARAN** is a poet and a bilingual translator of both Tamil and English poetry. She is the recipient of the SPARROW R Thyagarajan award for her poetry in Tamil and is a doctoral student in the Humanities at York University, Toronto.

**STEPHANIE SY-QUIA**'s debut, *Amnion*, will be published by Granta Poetry in November.

**JS TENNANT** studied languages and literature at Trinity College, Dublin, the University of Salamanca and Cambridge. He was poetry editor of *The White Review* 2011–2016. In 2020 he became the first English-language winner of the Michael Jacobs Award from the Gabriel García Márquez Foundation for Journalism.

**NATALIA TOLEDO**'s bilingual poetry (Zapotec-Spanish) has been translated into languages as varied as Nahuatl, Italian, and Punjabi. She serves as Under Secretary of Cultural Diversity and Literacy for Mexico.

**MARTÍN [JACINTO MEZA] TONALMEYOTL** is a Nahua poet and author of *Tlalkatsajtsilistle / Ritual de los olvidados* (2016), *Nosentlalilxochitlajtol / Antología personal* (2017), and *Istitsin ueyeatsintle / Uña mar* (2019).

**SHASH TREVETT** is a poet and a translator of Tamil poetry into English. She is currently a 2021 Visible Communities Translator in Residence at the National Centre for Writing and her pamphlet *From a Borrowed Land* is published by Smith|Doorstop.

**SARA URIBE** is a Mexican poet. Her most recent books are *Abroche su cinturón mientras esté sentado* (Filodecaballos, 2017) and *Antígona González*, translated by John Pluecker (Le Figues Press, 2016). Her work has been translated into English, German and French.

**KAREN MCCARTHY WOOLF**'s latest collection *Seasonal Disturbances* (Carcanet) was a winner in the inaugural Laurel Prize for Ecological Poetry. In 2020 she was a Fulbright Postdoctoral scholar at UCLA, where she was poet in residence at the Promise Institute for Human Rights.

**LIGIO ZANINI** (1927–1993) is a major Istriot poet of the late twentieth century. In 1948, Zanini, a schoolteacher, refused to take sides in the Yugoslav–Soviet Split and was arrested by secret police and sentenced to forced labour. On his release in 1952, Zanini was forbidden to teach. He published several collections, most notably, *Favalando cul cucal Filéipo in stu cantun da paradéisu* or *Conversations with Philip the seagull in this corner of paradise* (1979).